AQA
GCSE CHEMISTRY
A D D I T I O N S

Terry Mansfield

Hodder & Stoughton
A MEMBER OF THE HODDER HEADLINE GROUP

Contents

About this book

The contents

The contents of this book are designed to cover all aspects of the knowledge and understanding required by the AQA GCSE specifications in Chemistry (Co-ordinated) and Chemistry (Modular).

The subject content required by the KS4 Double Award specification for Materials and their properties attainment target is produced in a format identical to that used in the Hodder and Stoughton textbook *AQA GCSE Science*. This core material is supplemented by the additional subject content required for the specification in GCSE Chemistry.

What is in each chapter?

At the beginning of each chapter is a list of **key terms**. Where used for the first time, these key terms are emboldened. Some of the key terms are coloured. These are the extra terms you will need to know if you are going to be entered for the Higher tier papers in the final examination. All the key terms together with their meanings are also found in the **Glossary** on pages 74–77.

The contents of each chapter are divided into several **sections**. Each section concentrates on one topic. A symbol at the start of each section shows clearly which topic from the co-ordinated and modular courses is being targeted.

You will see a number of **Did you know?** boxes throughout each chapter. You will not have to learn the information in these boxes, but they are there to give extra interest to the topic.

At the end of various sections, you will find a number of **Topic Questions**. Because the topic questions have been designed to produce answers that you could use as a set of revision notes, it is recommended that you write down the questions as well as the answers. The questions written on a yellow background are the more demanding questions, expected to be answered if you are a grade B/A/A★ student. Don't worry if you have to re-read the topic again when you try to answer these questions. This will help you to learn the work.

At the end of each chapter is a **Summary**. The summary provides a brief analysis of the important points covered in the section.

Completing each chapter are some **GCSE questions** taken from past AQA (SEG) or past AQA (NEAB) examination papers. The questions written on a yellow background are the more demanding questions expected to be answered if you are a grade B/A/A★ student. Answering the GCSE questions will help give you an idea of what is wanted when you take your final science examination. Again, do not worry if you have to go back to read the work again. The examination questions may well test you on knowledge not included in the particular chapter. Don't worry – look through the other chapters to find the extra information you need to complete your answer.

Specification Matching Grid

Ideas and evidence in Science

Section	DA	Core/HT	Context
1.2	✓	core	Comparing the cost, efficiency and cleanliness of burning different fossil fuels
3.5	✓	core	How the contributions of Arrhenius, Lowry and Brønsted affected our understanding of acid-base behaviour.
3.5	✓	core	Why the work of Arrhenius took longer to be accepted than that of Lowry and Brønsted

Chapter 1

Organic chemistry

Key terms

addition polymerisation • addition reactions • alcohol • alkanes • alkenes • anaerobic • anion • biological catalyst • boiling point • bond energy • branched chain • carboxylic acids • cation • complete combustion • covalent • cross-linking bonds • double bonds • enzyme • ester • fermentation • functional group • general equation • general formula • haemoglobin • homologous series • hydrogenated • incomplete combustion • ionic • isomers • melting point • molecular formula • monomers • organic compounds • oxidise • plastics • polymer • relative molecular mass • saturated hydrocarbons • steroid • straight chain • structural formula • thermosetting plastics • thermosoftening plastics • unsaturated hydrocarbons • yeast

1.1

Co-ordinated	Modular
10.4	21 (14.6)

The meaning of 'organic compounds'

Most **organic compounds** come from living organisms but some can be made from inorganic materials. The compounds in crude oil, natural gas and coal are organic because they are the fossilised remains of living organisms. Living materials like wood also contain organic compounds.

All organic compounds contain the element carbon. Most of them also contain hydrogen and some contain other elements like oxygen, nitrogen, sulphur or the halogens.

Did you know?

Urea is a compound found in animal urine so it is an organic compound. It is used as a fertiliser and in the manufacture of certain types of polymers. But urea can also be manufactured commercially from the inorganic materials carbon dioxide and ammonia.

Figure 1.1
These substances – wood, coal and methylated spirit – are all organic

1

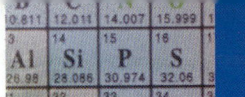

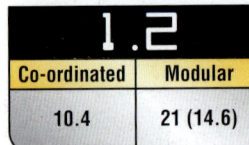

Co-ordinated	Modular
10.4	21 (14.6)

Burning organic compounds

When organic compounds are burned in air, the hydrogen is always **oxidised** to water.

If the air supply is plentiful, **complete combustion** takes place and the carbon is oxidised to carbon dioxide. But if the air supply is limited, **incomplete combustion** takes place and carbon monoxide and/or the element carbon are produced.

Carbon monoxide is highly poisonous because it combines with the **haemoglobin** in the blood and stops it from binding with oxygen. The body becomes starved of oxygen and this can lead to unconsciousness and death.

When incomplete combustion of an organic compound produces carbon, the small carbon particles get heated in the flame and glow. This makes the flame bright yellow. Once the particles are out of the flame they cool quickly and become black smoke. So a yellow, smoky flame is a sign of incomplete combustion.

With incomplete combustion, only some of the chemical energy from the organic compound is transferred to heat energy. Incomplete combustion is, therefore, inefficient compared with complete combustion.

When the air hole of a Bunsen burner is closed, there is not enough oxygen for the complete combustion of the gas. The flame is yellow and smoky and takes a long time to heat a beaker of water. Once the air hole is opened, air is sucked in the hole and complete combustion occurs. The resulting blue flame is much better at heating.

Figure 1.2

The yellow Bunsen flame shows incomplete combustion of the gas. The blue Bunsen flame shows complete combustion

The more carbon atoms a molecule has, the more oxygen is needed to oxidise it fully (see Figure 1.3).

Figure 1.3

The effect of carbon content on the colour of the flame

Compound	% carbon	Flame colour	Is combustion complete?	Is combustion efficient?
ethanol	52	blue	yes	yes
methane (natural gas)	75	blue or yellow	sometimes	varies
octane (in petrol)	84	yellow, smoky	no	no

The complete combustion of compounds with large organic molecules requires a lot of air. Specialised furnaces and boilers are needed to burn these compounds efficiently. In most cases this is not an economic situation. But in large factories and oil-powered ships that require a lot of energy, the process is economically sensible because the high cost of the boilers is offset by the much lower cost of the fuel.

In the home the commonly used fuels are coal, oil and natural gas. The table below gives some data on these fuels.

Fossil fuel	Approx. energy output (kJ/g)	Approx. mass of CO_2 per 1000 kJ of energy (grams)	Main pollutants produced	Relative cost of fuel for domestic heating Natural gas = 1
coal – lignite	17		smoke	
coal – anthracite	35	100	oxides of sulphur oxides of nitrogen	1.26
oil – petrol (gasoline)	50		oxides of nitrogen	
oil – paraffin (kerosene)	45	80		1.31
natural gas	90	60	oxides of nitrogen	1.00

Natural gas has several advantages over the other fuels. It produces more energy for the same mass of fuel and it produces less of the greenhouse gas carbon dioxide to get that energy. It is also considerably cheaper than the other fuels. Oil, though not as good as natural gas, is less polluting than coal. Oil does not have the high sulphur content of coal and it does not produce smoke. It also produces less carbon dioxide than coal to get the same amount of energy.

Equations for the combustion of methane

For the complete combustion of methane, the equation is:

$$CH_4 + 2O_2 \rightarrow CO_2 + 2H_2O$$

If combustion is incomplete, producing carbon monoxide, the equation is:

$$CH_4 + 1\tfrac{1}{2}O_2 \rightarrow CO + 2H_2O$$

The second equation needs less oxygen so it is the reaction that will occur when the oxygen supply is limited.

Organic compounds which contain nitrogen and chlorine, which are present in many polymers (plastics), burn to produce the toxic gases hydrogen cyanide (HCN) and hydrogen chloride (HCl), respectively. More of these gases is made if the air supply is limited.

Summary

◆ Compounds derived from living organisms are **organic compounds**.

◆ All organic compounds contain carbon. Most of them also contain hydrogen.

◆ When organic compounds are burned, the hydrogen is always **oxidised** to water.

◆ If **complete combustion** takes place, carbon is oxidised to carbon dioxide.

◆ If **incomplete combustion** takes place, carbon is oxidised to carbon monoxide.

◆ Some organic compounds contain nitrogen or chlorine. When they burn, toxic gases are produced.

Topic questions

1 What substances are formed when an organic compound burns completely in air?

2 Which of the following compounds would take most air for complete combustion?
   a) C_2H_6
   b) C_3H_6
   c) C_5H_{12}
   d) C_7H_{14}

3 Explain why the burning of some plastics produces toxic gases.

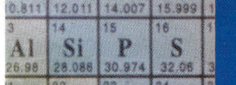

<table>
<tr><td>1.3</td><td></td></tr>
<tr><td>Co-ordinated</td><td>Modular</td></tr>
<tr><td>10.4</td><td>21 (14.7)</td></tr>
</table>

Homologous series

An **homologous series** is a family of compounds with similar structures and chemical properties. All members of an homologous series have the same **general formula**. The alkanes, alkenes, alcohols and carboxylic acids are examples of homologous series.

The alkanes

The general formula of the **alkanes** is C_nH_{2n+2}. All alkanes are flammable but otherwise are fairly unreactive.

Figure 1.4 shows the **structural formulae** of some alkanes. The similarity of the structures is clear.

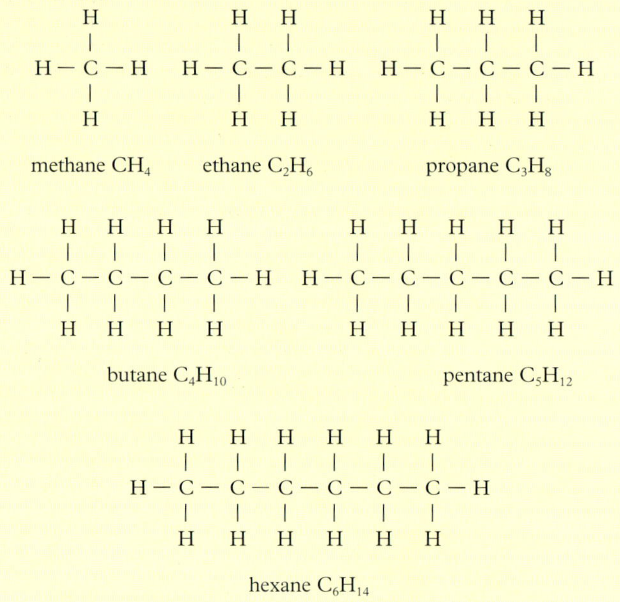

Figure 1.4
The structural formulae of the first six alkanes

$$
\begin{array}{cccc}
& H & H\ \ H & H\ \ H\ \ H \\
& | & |\ \ | & |\ \ |\ \ | \\
H-&C-H\quad & H-C-C-H\quad & H-C-C-C-H \\
& | & |\ \ | & |\ \ |\ \ | \\
& H & H\ \ H & H\ \ H\ \ H
\end{array}
$$

methane CH_4 ethane C_2H_6 propane C_3H_8

$$
\begin{array}{cc}
H\ \ H\ \ H\ \ H & H\ \ H\ \ H\ \ H\ \ H \\
|\ \ |\ \ |\ \ | & |\ \ |\ \ |\ \ |\ \ | \\
H-C-C-C-C-H & H-C-C-C-C-C-H \\
|\ \ |\ \ |\ \ | & |\ \ |\ \ |\ \ |\ \ | \\
H\ \ H\ \ H\ \ H & H\ \ H\ \ H\ \ H\ \ H
\end{array}
$$

butane C_4H_{10} pentane C_5H_{12}

$$
\begin{array}{c}
H\ \ H\ \ H\ \ H\ \ H\ \ H \\
|\ \ |\ \ |\ \ |\ \ |\ \ | \\
H-C-C-C-C-C-C-H \\
|\ \ |\ \ |\ \ |\ \ |\ \ | \\
H\ \ H\ \ H\ \ H\ \ H\ \ H
\end{array}
$$

hexane C_6H_{14}

The alkanes have no **double bonds**. For this reason they are known as **saturated hydrocarbons**, as no more atoms can bond to the carbons.

The **general equation** for the complete combustion of the alkanes is:

$$C_nH_{2n+2} + \tfrac{1}{2}(3n+1)O_2 \rightarrow nCO_2 + (n+1)H_2O$$

For methane, where n = 1, the formula becomes:

$$CH_4 + 2O_2 \rightarrow CO_2 + 2H_2O$$

And for ethane, where n = 2, the formula becomes:

$$C_2H_6 + 3\tfrac{1}{2}O_2 \rightarrow 2CO_2 + 3H_2O$$

The general equation for the incomplete combustion of alkanes to produce carbon monoxide is:

$$C_nH_{2n+2} + (n+\tfrac{1}{2})O_2 \rightarrow nCO + (n+1)H_2O$$

For methane, where n = 1, the formula becomes:

$$CH_4 + 1\tfrac{1}{2}O_2 \rightarrow CO + 2H_2O$$

And for ethane, where n = 2, the formula becomes:

$$C_2H_6 + 2\tfrac{1}{2}O_2 \rightarrow 2CO + 3H_2O$$

Did you know?

Air is about 20% oxygen so for every millilitre of oxygen required to burn an alkane, 5 millilitres of air are required. For an alkane of formula C_nH_{2n+2}, the amount of oxygen required for the complete combustion of 1 millilitre of the alkane vapour is $\frac{1}{2} \times (3n+1)$. This means that $2\frac{1}{2} \times (3n+1)$ millilitres of air is required.

Alkane	Millilitres of air to burn 1 millilitre of alkane vapour
methane	10
ethane	17.5
propane	25
butane	32.5
pentane	40

To burn 1 millilitre of petrol vapour requires between 60 and 70 millilitres of air. Technical problems make it impossible to run at this ratio. In car engines the mixture has a much higher petrol content than the theoretical value. This means the combustion is incomplete and the products include significant amounts of carbon monoxide. Catalytic converters change most of this back to carbon dioxide before it is released into the atmosphere.

The alkenes

The general formula of the **alkenes** is C_nH_{2n}. Alkanes are flammable and are generally more reactive than alkanes

Figure 1.5
The structural formulae of the first four alkenes

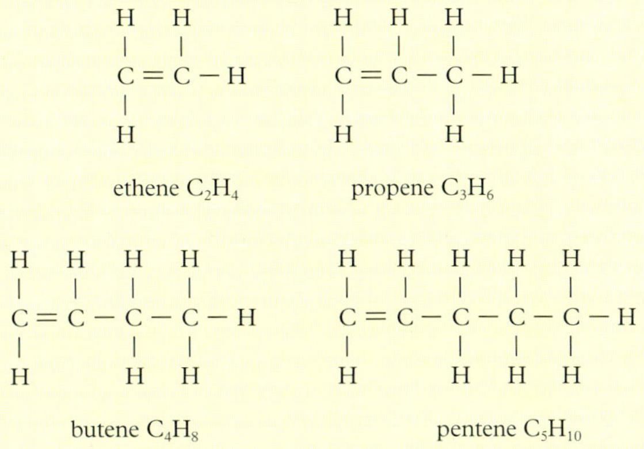

The similarity of the structures is clear from Figure 1.5.

The alkenes have one double bond. For this reason they are known as **unsaturated hydrocarbons**. They are more reactive than the alkanes because of the double bond.

A double bond is shorter and therefore stronger than a single bond. It may seem strange that it is the double bond which is the part of the molecule that is attacked by reactants. The reason is that the two bonds in a double bond are not identical. The second bond is much weaker than the first. The **bond energy** of a single bond (C–C) is 340 kJ mol^{-1}; for a double bond (C = C) the bond energy is 610 kJ mol^{-1}. Clearly the double bond is stronger than a single bond but the second bond has a bond energy of 610 – 340 = 270 kJ mol^{-1}. The second bond has only about 80% of the strength of the first bond.

All the reactions of the alkenes (apart from combustion) are **addition reactions** where some substance attacks the double bond. There are three important reactions.

1 The addition of hydrogen to form an alkane

Using the example of ethene:

$$C_2H_4 + H_2 \rightarrow C_2H_6$$

This reaction is used commercially to convert vegetable oils to margarine. Vegetable oils are liquids. They contain unsaturated chains of carbon atoms. Reacting the oil with hydrogen (using a suitable catalyst) will cause some of the double bonds to be **hydrogenated**. This process converts the oil to a solid.

Figure 1.6
Liquid vegetable oil is hydrogenated to produce solid margarine

Did you know?

Unsaturated fats (like vegetable oils) are less harmful to your health than saturated fats (animal fats). Converting unsaturated vegetable oils to saturated fats to make margarine increases the danger to health.

Food labels indicate what percentage of the fat they contain is saturated fat and what percentage is unsaturated fat.

2 The addition of bromine to form a dibromoalkane

Again using the example of ethene:

$C_2H_4 + Br_2(aq) \rightarrow C_2H_4Br_2$ (more usually written as) $CH_2Br.CH_2Br$

This reaction can be used to tell the difference between alkanes and alkenes. An alkane will not react with bromine water (bromine dissolved in water) but an alkene will. If bromine water is shaken with an alkane, the bromine water remains brown but if shaken with an alkene it is decolourised.

Figure 1.7
When an alkene is shaken with bromine water, it will decolourise it

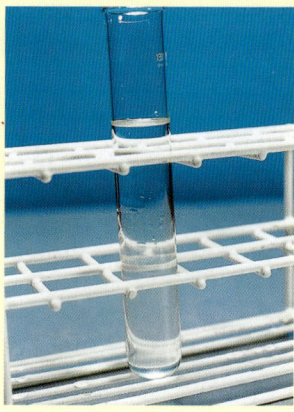

3 Addition with itself to form a polymer (This is dealt with later.)

Figure 1.8 shows how the attacking substance opens up the double bond. You can see from this diagram why dibromoethane is written as $CH_2Br.CH_2Br$ instead of $C_2H_4Br_2$.

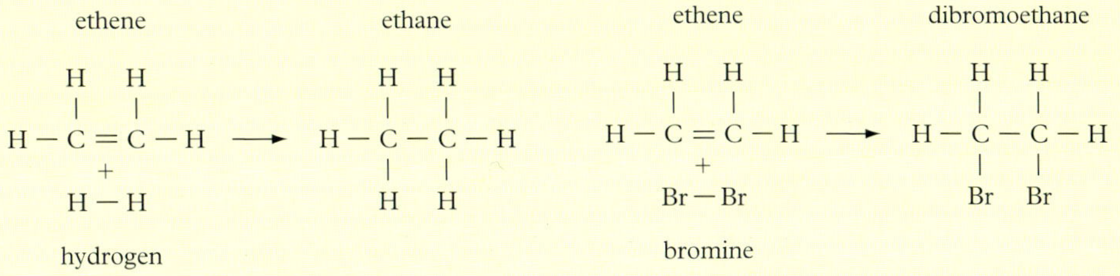

Figure 1.8
The addition reactions of alkenes

Did you know?

The main reason why dibromoethane is written as $CH_2Br.CH_2Br$ instead of $C_2H_4Br_2$ is that there are two dibromoethanes. One with a bromine on each carbon atom; the other with both bromine atoms on the same carbon atom. They are written as $CH_2Br.CH_2Br$ and $CHBr_2.CH_3$ to tell them apart.

They also have different names. $CHBr_2.CH_3$ is called 1,1-dibromoethane (because both bromine atoms are on the same carbon atom) and $CH_2Br.CH_2Br$ is called 1,2-dibromethane (because one bromine atom is on the 1st carbon atom and the other is on the 2nd carbon atom.)

Did you know?

Hydrocarbons containing halogen atoms are used as anaesthetics. One of the earliest anaesthetics was trichloromethane, $CHCl_3$, commonly known as chloroform. More recent anaesthetics include halothane, sometimes called flurothane, $CF_3.CHBrCl$. One of the advantages of these anaesthetics is that they are non-flammable.

The combustion of alkenes is not an addition reaction. Combustion results in the whole molecule being destroyed.

The general equation for the complete combustion of the alkenes is:

$$C_nH_{2n} + 1\tfrac{1}{2}nO_2 \rightarrow nCO_2 + nH_2O$$

And for ethene, where n = 2, the formula becomes:

$$C_2H_4 + 3O_2 \rightarrow 2CO_2 + 2H_2O$$

The general equation for the incomplete combustion of alkenes is:

$$C_nH_{2n} + nO_2 \rightarrow nCO + nH_2O$$

And for ethene, where n = 2, the formula becomes:

$$C_2H_4 + 2O_2 \rightarrow 2CO + 2H_2O$$

Summary

◆ An **homologous series** is a family of compounds with similar structures and chemical properties.

◆ Alkanes, alkenes, alcohols and carboxylic acids are all examples of homologous series.

◆ **Alkanes** have the general formula C_nH_{2n+2}.

◆ Alkanes are **saturated hydrocarbons** because they only have C–C single bonds.

◆ Alkanes are flammable but are otherwise unreactive.

◆ **Alkenes** have the general formula C_nH_{2n}.

◆ Alkenes are **unsaturated hydrocarbons** because they contain a C = C double bond.

◆ Alkenes are flammable and are more reactive than alkanes. They will react with hydrogen, bromine and water (steam). In each case the double bond is attacked.

◆ Alkenes can **polymerise**.

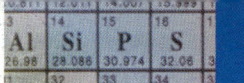

1.4

Co-ordinated	Modular
10.4	21 (14.7)

Isomerism

The alkanes in Figure 1.4 are all 'straight chain' alkanes. Not all alkanes are straight chains, some exist as 'branched chains'. Figure 1.9 shows two alkanes. One is a straight chain alkane (butane), the other is a branched chain alkane. The branched chain alkane has the same formula as butane but a different structure. It also has different physical properties from butane. It is called 2-methylpropane to distinguish it from butane.

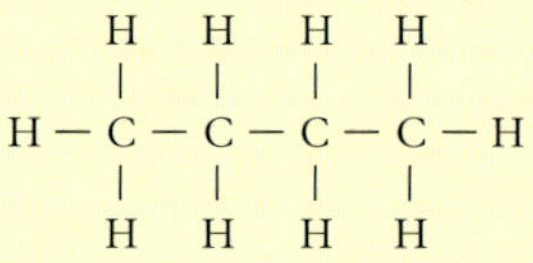

Figure 1.9
The isomers of butane

$$H-\overset{\displaystyle H}{\underset{\displaystyle H}{C}}-\overset{\displaystyle H}{\underset{\displaystyle H}{C}}-\overset{\displaystyle H}{\underset{\displaystyle H}{C}}-\overset{\displaystyle H}{\underset{\displaystyle H}{C}}-H$$

butane C_4H_{10}

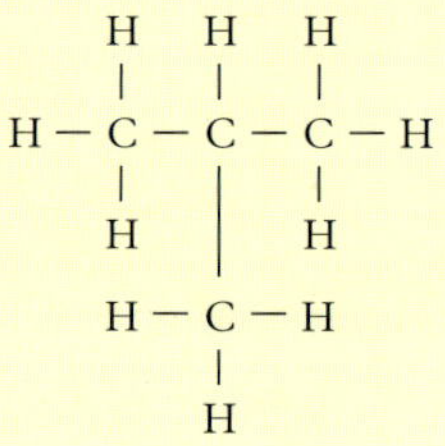

2-methylpropane
(isomer of butane C_4H_{10})

Organic compounds with the same **molecular formula** (and same **relative molecular mass**) are called **isomers**. Butane (C_4H_{10}) and 2-methylpropane (C_4H_{10}) are isomers.

Naming isomers

The names of isomers are worked out using the following rules:

Rule for naming isomer	Rule applied to the isomer of butane
1 a) Find the longest chain of carbon atoms.	3 C atoms
b) What is the name of the alkane with this number of carbon atoms?	propane
2 To which carbon atom is/are the branch(es) bonded? Count from the end to make the number/s as small as possible.	2
3 Name the branch by dropping the '–ane' ending and replacing it by '–yl'.	1 carbon atom (would be methane) so methyl
4 Put the parts of the name together in the sequence Rule 2, Rule 3, Rule 1. Put a hyphen between the number and the name. Join the two parts of the name to make one word.	2-methylpropane

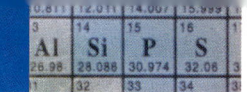

The isomers of pentane

Figure 1.10 show the three isomers of pentane. Check to see how the rules are applied in this example.

Figure 1.10

The structural formulae of the isomers of pentane

```
    H   H   H   H   H                    H   H   H   H                      H
    |   |   |   |   |                    |   |   |   |                      |
H — C — C — C — C — C — H        H — C — C — C — C — H              H — C — H
    |   |   |   |   |                    |   |   |   |                  H   |   H
    H   H   H   H   H                    H   |   H   H                  |   |   |
                                             |                     H — C — C — C — H
   pentane C₅H₁₂                         H — C — H                     |   |   |
                                             |                         H   |   H
                                             H                             |
                                                                      H — C — H
                                        2-methylbutane                     |
                                                                           H

                                                                  2,2-dimethylpropane
```

Figure 1.11

Why there is not another isomer of pentane

```
    H   H   H   H                        │       H   H   H   H
    |   |   |   |                        │       |   |   |   |
H — C — C — C — C — H                     │   H — C — C — C — C — H
    |   |   |   |                        │       |   |   |   |
    H   |   H   H                        │       H   H   |   H
        |                                │               |
    H — C — H                            │           H — C — H
        |                                │               |
        H                                │               H

   2-methylbutane                     MIRROR          2-methylbutane
```

It is easy to think that there might be another isomer of pentane. Figure 1.11 shows why this is not the case. The isomer that looks as if it ought to be 3-methylpropane is just a mirror image of 2-methylpropane. When you are looking for isomers you must take care not to make this mistake. It is easy to make this mistake because structural formulae are two-dimensional and the molecules are three-dimensional. Figure 1.12 is a more accurate picture of the true shape of the three isomers of pentane.

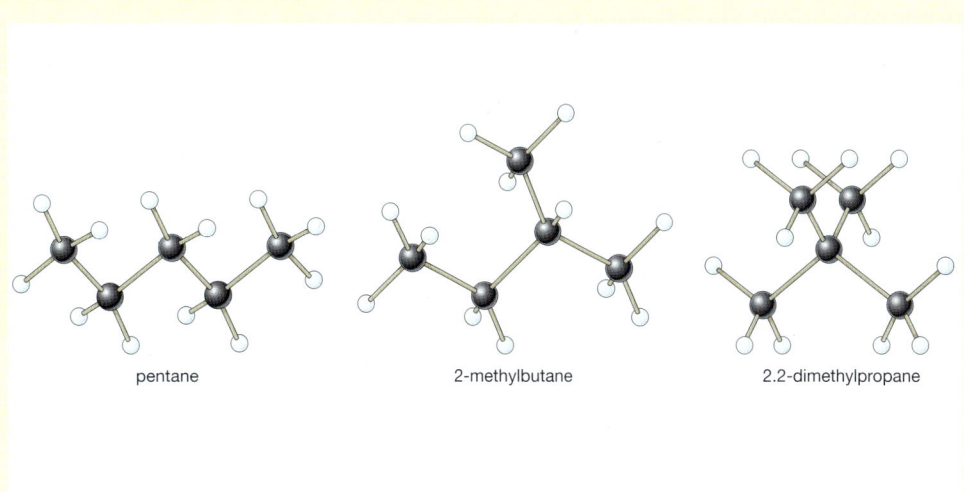

pentane   2-methylbutane   2.2-dimethylpropane

Figure 1.12

Ball and stick representations of the isomers of pentane

Summary

◆ **Isomers** are substances with the same molecular formula but different chemical structures.

◆ Isomers have different physical (and often chemical) properties.

1.5 The physical properties of alkanes

Co-ordinated	Modular
10.4	21 (14.7)

Figure 1.13
Table of melting points and boiling points for the first 10 alkanes

The **melting points** and **boiling points** of the alkanes increase as the number of carbon atoms increases.

Name of alkane	Number of carbon atoms	Melting point / °C	Boiling point / °C
methane	1	−182	−164
ethane	2	−183	−89
propane	3	−190	−42
butane	4	−138	−1
pentane	5	−130	36
hexane	6	−95	69
heptane	7	−91	98
octane	8	−57	126
nonane	9	−51	151
decane	10	−30	174

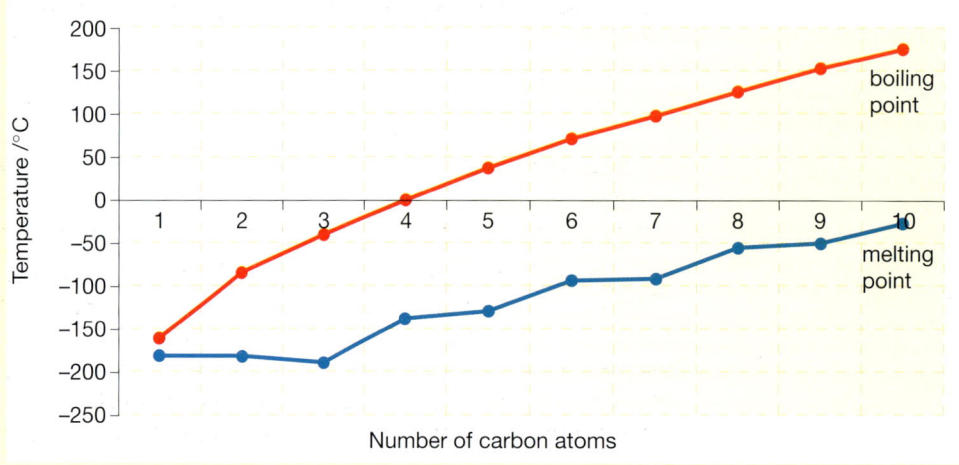

Figure 1.14
Graph of melting points and boiling points for the first 10 alkanes

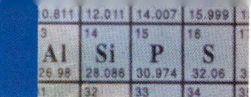
The melting points have an irregular trend but the boiling points show a very clear pattern of behaviour.

Alkane molecules have a slight attraction for each other. Weak forces hold the molecules together. The longer the molecule, the more contact there is between molecules and the stronger the forces holding the molecules together (see Figure 1.15). This means that more energy is needed to overcome these forces and change the alkane into a gas. So the longer the molecule, the higher the boiling point.

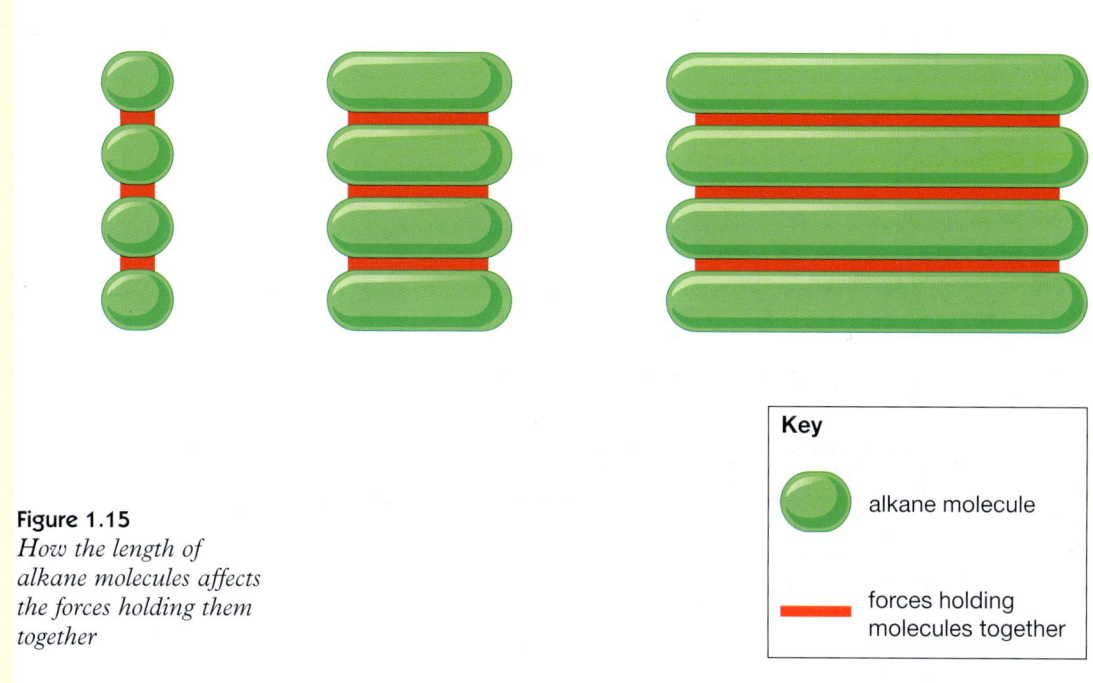

Key

alkane molecule

forces holding molecules together

Figure 1.15
How the length of alkane molecules affects the forces holding them together

Physical properties of isomers

Although the chemical properties of the isomers of alkanes are quite similar, their physical properties are not. Figure 1.16 shows the boiling points of the isomers of butane and pentane.

Figure 1.16
The boiling points of the isomers of butane and pentane

Alkane	Boiling point / °C
butane	−1
2-methylpropane	−12
pentane	36
2-methylbutane	28
2,2-dimethylpropane	10

Branched chain alkanes have lower boiling points than their straight chain isomer. The more branched a chain is, the lower its boiling point. Figure 1.12 shows how the structures of the isomers of pentane differ. The molecules of branched chain alkanes cannot get as close together as those of straight chain alkanes. This means the forces holding the molecules together are weaker; less energy is needed to separate the molecules so the boiling point of the compound will be lower.

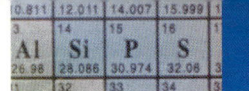

Figure 1.17
How branching in alkane molecules affects the forces holding them together

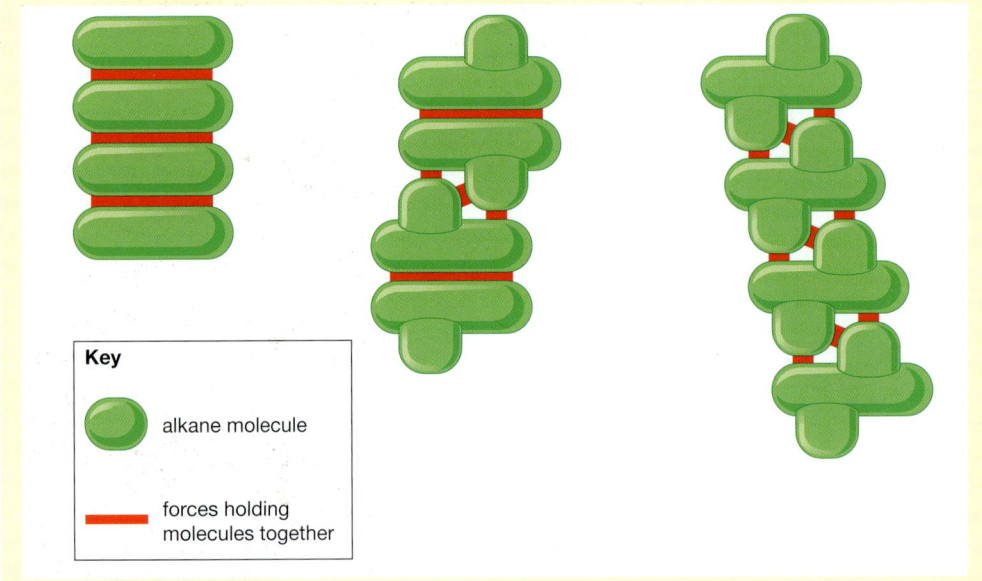

Key

 alkane molecule

 forces holding molecules together

Topic questions

1 a) What is the general formula of an alkene?
 b) What is the chemical equation for the complete combustion of ethene?

2 a) Write a word equation for:
   i) the complete combustion of methane.
   ii) the incomplete combustion of propene to produce carbon monoxide.
 b) Write a balanced chemical equation for each of these word equations.

3 Explain, using bond energies, why alkenes are more reactive than alkanes.

4 Give **three** examples of addition reactions of alkenes.

5 Name the five isomers of hexane and draw the structural formulae.

6 Explain why the boiling point of pentane is:
 a) higher than that of butane
 b) higher than that of 2-methylbutane.

Summary

◆ The melting points of alkanes generally increase as the number of carbon atoms increases.

◆ The boiling points of alkanes increase in a regular way as the number of carbon atoms increases.

1.6 Alcohols

Co-ordinated	Modular
10.4	21 (14.8)

Ethanol

Ethanol is the **alcohol** that is present in alcoholic drinks. It is made by the **fermentation** of sugars in the presence of yeast.

$$C_6H_{12}O_6 \rightarrow 2C_2H_5OH + 2CO_2$$

glucose → ethanol + carbon dioxide

Yeast produces an **enzyme** (zymase) which is a **biological catalyst** for the reaction. In the fermentation process, the raw materials are mixed with water and yeast and left at a temperature slightly higher than room temperature. The reaction is **anaerobic** so air is excluded.

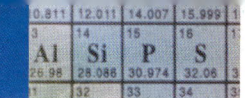

Figure 1.18 shows a 'home brewing' apparatus. The airlock in the bung prevents air getting into the bottle. The ethanol produced poisons the yeast and eventually the reaction stops. Once the reaction has stopped, the ethanol can be removed from the mixture by fractional distillation.

Figure 1.18
Home brewing apparatus

Did you know?

Spirits like whisky and brandy are made by the fractional distillation of wines and ales. The first substance distilled off is methanol (boiling point 64°C). This is a toxic alcohol so must be removed from the mixture. (It is sold for industrial use.) The second substance is ethanol (boiling point 78°C). This is kept. Finally the water is distilled off and discarded. The flavours and colours of the original material remain and these are blended with the ethanol to produce spirits.

Ethanol is used as a solvent and as a fuel. In some third world countries where the cost of oil is high, ethanol, made by fermenting crops like sugar cane, is added to petrol to produce a fuel called gasohol. Ethanol is a good fuel because it burns readily with a blue, non-smoky flame.

In industry, ethanol is also made from ethene.

ethene C_2H_4 　　　　　　　ethanol C_2H_5OH

```
      H   H                        H   H
      |   |                        |   |
  H — C = C — H      ⟶       H — C — C — H
          +                        |   |
      H — O                        H   OH
          |
          H

    water        ↘           ↗
                  H   H
                  |   |
              H — C ═ C — H
                    +
                  H ┄ O
                      |
                      H
```

The equation shows how water (as steam) can be added to the double bond. The process requires temperatures of about 300°C and pressures of about 65 atmospheres (6500 kPa). Phosphoric acid is used as a catalyst.

Advantages and disadvantages of the two methods of making alcohol

When there are two methods of producing a chemical, there is competition between these methods. Usually the cheaper method is favoured. This is why the industrial manufacture of chemicals always uses the cheapest possible raw material. If two methods are available and both are used it is because there are advantages and disadvantages in each method so neither is the 'winner'.

The table below analyses the advantages and disadvantages of each method of making ethanol.

Figure 1.19
Comparing the advantages and disadvantages of the two methods of preparing ethanol

Factor considered	Method	
	Fermentation	Ethene + water
Rate of production (rate of reaction)	Comparatively slow. Takes some weeks for the mixture to ferment fully.	Relatively fast
Quality of the product	After fractional distillation is about 96% pure ethanol. (The impurity is water.)	Not very pure. The product is not suitable for consumption or medical purposes.
Manufacturing process	Produced in batches. Batch processes are not very efficient and industry tries to avoid them.	Continuous production. Reactants enter one end of the plant and products emerge from the other continuously.
Use of resources	Uses sustainable resources. Yeast is a living organism and reproduces. Plant material used can be grown.	Uses finite resources. Ethene is obtained from oil.

The cells shaded grey are for the process which has the advantage.

No reference is made in the table to the energy costs. The fermentation process uses very little energy until the fractional distillation stage. The other process uses energy to produce steam to heat the reaction vessel to a high temperature and to pressurise the reactants.

The homologous series of the alcohols

Alcohols form an homologous series. The general formula is $C_nH_{2n+1}OH$. Notice that the H symbols are not all together. This is to show that ethanol has an –OH group attached to it. The –OH group is an example of a functional group. Substances with the –OH functional group have similar chemical reactions because of that group.

Alcohols are named systematically. The alkane with one carbon atom is called methane and the alcohol with one carbon atom is called methanol.

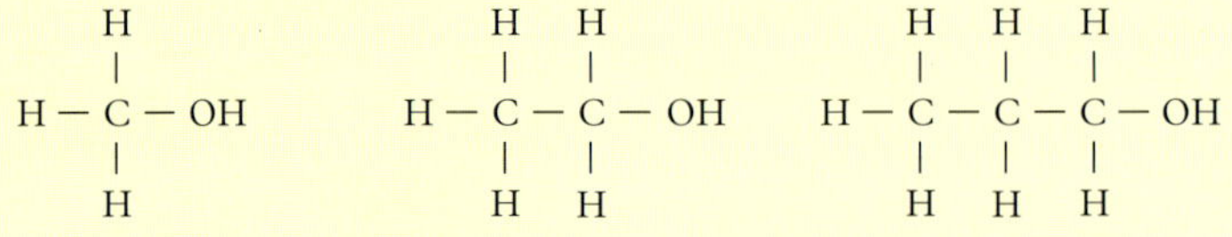

Figure 1.20
Some members of the homologous series of alcohols

methanol CH_3OH　　ethanol C_2H_5OH　　propanol C_3H_7OH

Did you know?

Isomerism also occurs in alcohols.

$$
\begin{array}{ccc}
\text{H} & \text{H} & \text{H} \\
| & | & | \\
\text{H} - \text{C} - \text{C} - \text{C} - \text{H} \\
| & | & | \\
\text{H} & \text{H} & \text{OH}
\end{array}
\qquad
\text{II}
\begin{array}{ccc}
\text{H} & \text{H} & \text{H} \\
| & | & | \\
\text{C} - \text{C} - \text{C} - \text{H} \\
| & | & | \\
\text{H} & \text{OH} & \text{H}
\end{array}
$$

In each case the chains are straight chains but the functional –OH group is situated on a different carbon atom. The chemical and physical properties of these two alcohols will be slightly different.

The naming system is similar to that used in naming branched chain alkanes. They are called propan-1-ol and propan-2-ol, respectively.

The **steroid**, cholesterol, contains the –OH functional group. Cholesterol is an essential steroid for humans but too much of it can cause heart disease.

The chemical reactions of alcohols

All alcohols are flammable. The products of complete combustion are carbon dioxide and water (steam). For ethanol the reaction is:

$$C_2H_5OH + 3O_2 \rightarrow 3H_2O + 2CO_2$$

Alcohols also react with sodium to form hydrogen. This reaction occurs because of the presence of the –OH functional group. The reaction shown is for ethanol but it also works equally well with other alcohols.

$$2Na + 2C_2H_5OH \rightarrow 2C_2H_5ONa + H_2$$

The product C_2H_5ONa is called sodium ethoxide. It is an ionic compound. This is the first **ionic** compound mentioned in this chapter. This is because the bonds in organic compounds are almost entirely **covalent**.

Topic questions

1 Which of the following is the formula of ethanol?
   a) CH_3OH
   b) C_2H_4
   c) C_2H_5OH
   d) C_2H_6

2 In some parts of the world alcohol is added to petrol to make a fuel for vehicles. Which method of alcohol manufacture is used? Explain why this method is used.

3 Write a balanced chemical equation for the reaction of sodium with methanol. Name the products of the reaction.

Summary

◆ **Alcohols** contain the –OH **functional group**.

◆ **Ethanol** can be made by the **fermentation** of sugar by the enzymes in **yeast** or by the addition of water (steam) across the double bond of ethene. There are advantages and disadvantages with either method of preparation.

◆ Ethanol reacts with sodium to form sodium ethoxide. Other alcohols react with sodium in a similar way.

1.7

Co-ordinated	Modular
10.4	21 (14.9)

Carboxylic acids

Carboxylic acids also form an homologous series. Figure 1.14 shows some of the members of that series.

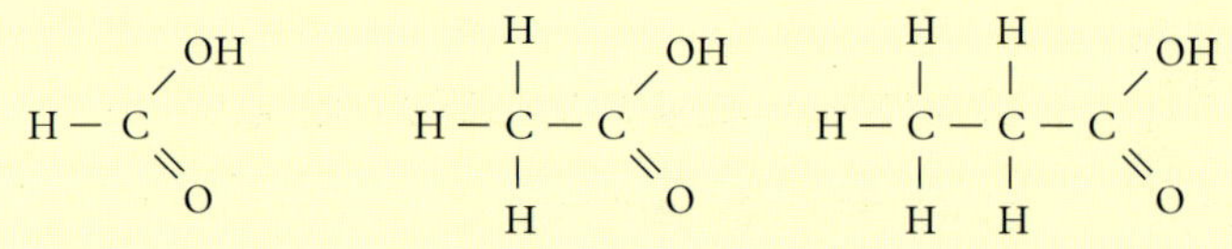

Figure 1.21

The first three members of the homologous series of carboxylic acids

methanoic acid
H.COOH

ethanoic acid
$CH_3.COOH$

propanoic acid
$C_2H_5.COOH$

In carboxylic acids the functional group is –COOH.

The reactions of carboxylic acids

All carboxylic acids are weak acids (see Chapter 3). This is because the –O–H bond in the –COOH functional group is slightly ionised. They have typical acidic behaviours. They are neutralised by alkalis and they react with carbonates and hydrogencarbonates to produce carbon dioxide. In each of these reactions a carboxylic acid salt is produced.

For example:

$$H.COOH + NaOH \rightarrow H_2O + H.COONa$$

methanoic acid + sodium hydroxide → water + sodium methanoate

$$2CH_3.COOH + Na_2CO_3 \rightarrow CO_2 + H_2O + 2CH_3.COONa$$

ethanoic acid + sodium carbonate → carbon dioxide + water + sodium ethanoate

$$C_2H_5.COOH + NaHCO_3 \rightarrow CO_2 + H_2O + C_2H_5.COONa$$

propanoic acid + sodium hydrogencarbonate → carbon dioxide + water + sodium propanoate

The salts produced are ionic, so $C_2H_5.COONa$ could be written $C_2H_5.COO^- Na^+$.

Notice that the formulae for salts of carboxylic acids are written 'backwards'. The **anion** (negative ion) is written first followed by the **cation** (positive ion). This is the conventional way of writing the formulae of organic salts. But there is nothing wrong in writing them with the positive ion first (e.g. $Na^+C_2H_5.COO^-$).

In carboxylic acids it is only the hydrogen in the –COOH functional group that is replaced. This is because the OH bond in the –COOH functional group is partly ionic but the –C–H bonds are all covalent.

Carboxylic acids will react with alcohols. The products are called **esters**. The reaction is reversible and very slow. Concentrated sulphuric acid is used as a catalyst for this reaction.

$$CH_3.COOH + C_2H_5OH \rightleftharpoons CH_3.COO.C_2H_5 + H_2O$$

ethanoic acid + ethanol ⇌ ethyl ethanoate + water

Although this reaction seems similar to the reaction between a carboxylic acid and an alkali, it is wrong to think of the reaction like this. Alcohols are not at all like alkalis and esters do not behave like salts. All salts have ions; all esters are covalently bonded. Esters have characteristic odours and flavours and are used as fragrances and food flavourings.

Uses of carboxylic acids

Ethanoic acid (probably the first acid ever used by man) is obtained by the oxidation of ethanol. It is the acid present in vinegar and in 'sour' alcoholic drinks. Ethanoic acid is also used in the manufacture of the fibre, acetate rayon.

Other common carboxylic acids include:

- citric acid, present in citrus fruits like oranges, lemons, limes and grapefruit and used as an additive in many soft drinks

- ethanoylsalicylic acid (better known as 'aspirin') used in the relief of pain and to 'thin' the blood of people at risk of heart attacks

- ascorbic acid (vitamin C) present in fresh fruit and vegetables.

Figure 1.22
All these things contain common carboxylic acids

Topic questions

1 Which functional group is present in all carboxylic acids?

2 Give **three** examples of reactions where carboxylic acids behave as typical acids. Write a balanced chemical equation to illustrate each reaction.

3 a) Write a chemical equation for the reaction of propanoic acid with methanol. Name the products of the reaction.
   b) The organic compound produced in a) is an isomer of ethyl ethanoate.
      i) What is meant by the word 'isomer'?
      ii) Use diagrams of the structures to explain why the organic compound produced in a) and ethyl ethanoate are different compounds.

Summary

- **Carboxylic acids** contain the –COOH functional group.

- Carboxylic acids are weak acids. They have typical acid behaviour – they can be neutralised by alkalis and react with carbonates and hydrogencarbonates to produce carbon dioxide.

- Carboxylic acids react with alcohols to form **esters**. This is a **reversible reaction**.

1.8 Polymers

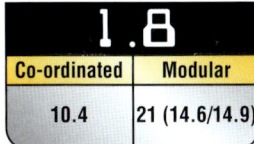

Co-ordinated	Modular
10.4	21 (14.6/14.9)

The structure of polymers

Polymers are the substances generally called **plastics**. They are made of long molecules in the form of chains. The atoms in these molecules are held together with strong covalent bonds. The molecules are tangled together and joined to each other by **cross-linking bonds**.

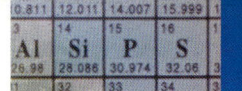
Figure 1.23
The arrangement of molecules in a polymer

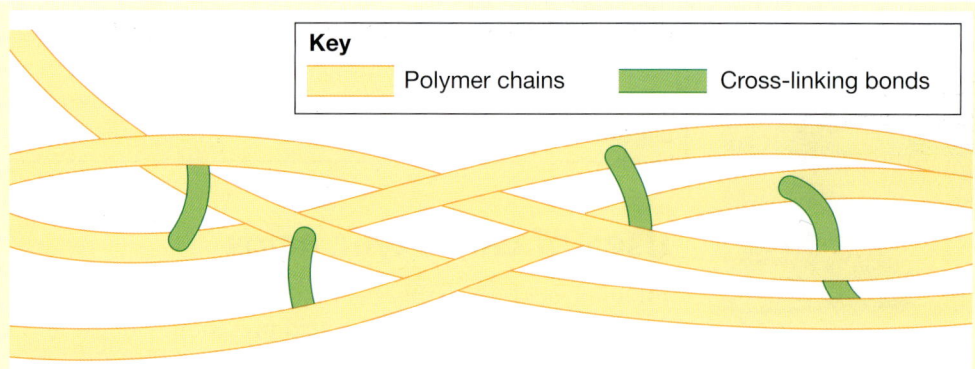

Formation of polymers

Most polymers are made from compounds containing the $-C=C-$ bond These compounds can link together because of the double bond. The process of linking these bonds together is called **addition polymerisation**. The individual molecules that join together are called **monomers**. So molecules of the monomer ethene will link together to form the polymer poly(ethene) (often called polythene) and the monomer propene will form the polymer poly(propene) (often called polypropylene). The monomer chloroethene ($CH_2=CHCl$) polymerises to poly(chloroethene) usually called polyvinylchloride or PVC.

The equation for the polymerisation of ethene is:

$$nCH_2=CH_2 \rightarrow [-CH_2-CH_2-]_n$$

Figure 1.24 shows the way ethene polymerises.

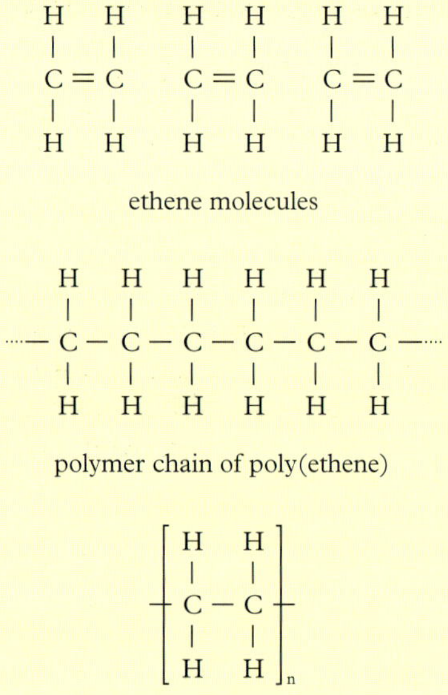

Figure 1.24
Polymerisation of ethene to form poly(ethene)

$$
\begin{array}{cccccc}
H & H & H & H & H & H \\
| & | & | & | & | & | \\
C & = C & C & = C & C & = C \\
| & | & | & | & | & | \\
H & H & H & H & H & H
\end{array}
$$

ethene molecules

$$
\begin{array}{cccccc}
H & H & H & H & H & H \\
| & | & | & | & | & | \\
\cdots- C & - C & - C & - C & - C & - C -\cdots \\
| & | & | & | & | & | \\
H & H & H & H & H & H
\end{array}
$$

polymer chain of poly(ethene)

$$
\left[
\begin{array}{cc}
H & H \\
| & | \\
C & - C \\
| & | \\
H & H
\end{array}
\right]_n
$$

representation of poly(ethene) molecule

Did you know?

The polymerisation process is quite complex. Poly(ethene) exists in two forms, low density poly(ethene) and high density poly(ethene). The low density form requires a pressure of about 2000 atmospheres and temperature of about 250°C. The high density form is manufactured at atmospheric pressure and a temperature of about 100°C but requires a complex combination of catalysts and is more expensive to produce.

Figure 1.25 shows the polymerisation of chloroethene to form PVC.

Figure 1.25
*How monomers of
chloroethene link to form
PVC*

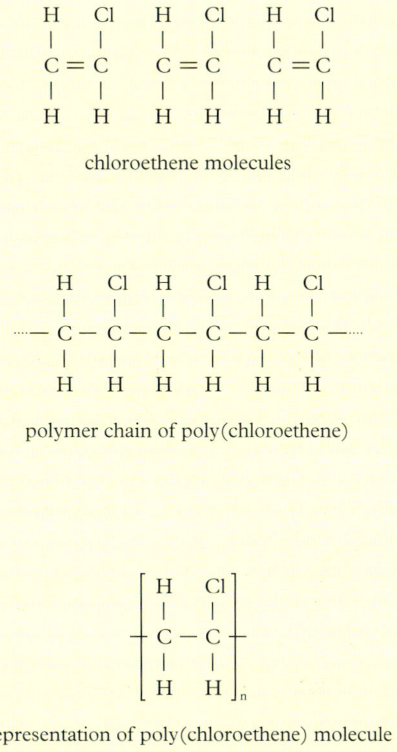

$$
\begin{array}{cccccc}
H & Cl & H & Cl & H & Cl \\
| & | & | & | & | & | \\
C & = C & C & = C & C & = C \\
| & | & | & | & | & | \\
H & H & H & H & H & H
\end{array}
$$

chloroethene molecules

$$
\begin{array}{cccccc}
H & Cl & H & Cl & H & Cl \\
| & | & | & | & | & | \\
\cdots\!-C & - C & - C & - C & - C & - C -\!\cdots \\
| & | & | & | & | & | \\
H & H & H & H & H & H
\end{array}
$$

polymer chain of poly(chloroethene)

$$
\left[
\begin{array}{cc}
H & Cl \\
| & | \\
C & - C \\
| & | \\
H & H
\end{array}
\right]_n
$$

representation of poly(chloroethene) molecule

Thermosoftening and thermosetting plastics

Poly(ethene), poly(propene) and PVC are **thermosoftening plastics**.
Thermosoftening plastics have weak cross-linking bonds. These bonds are easily
broken by heat and the polymer can be reshaped. When it cools, new cross-link
bonds form. This means that thermosoftening plastics can easily be moulded into
shape.

Thermosetting plastics are polymers in which the cross-linking bonds are formed
when the material is heated. These bonds are very much stronger than those in
thermosoftening plastics. Heating cannot reshape thermosetting plastics. The
plastic Melamine (used in the manufacture of furniture) is an example of a
thermosetting polymer. Many glues are thermosetting polymers.

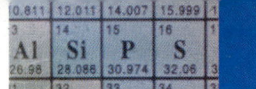
Topic questions

1 The structural formula of propene is:

```
        H   H
        |   |
        C = C     H
        |     \  /
        H      C
              / \
             H   H
```

Draw the structural formula of poly(propene).

2 Electric switches and sockets are made from plastic.
   a) Why is this safer than making them from metal?
   b) Is the plastic used thermosoftening or thermosetting? Explain why that type of plastic is used.

3 What is the name of the monomer used to make poly(styrene)?

Summary

◆ **Polymers** are formed when **monomer** alkenes bond together.

◆ Polymers can be **thermosoftening** or **thermosetting**.

Examination questions

1 Cars in Brazil use ethanol as a fuel instead of petrol (octane). The ethanol is produced by the fermentation of sugar solution from sugar cane.
   a) What must be added to sugar solution to make it ferment?   *(1 mark)*
   b) Which is the most suitable temperature for a fermentation.

   0°C   10°C   30°C   70°C   100°C
                                              (1 mark)
   c) i) What compounds are formed by the complete combustion of ethanol?   *(2 marks)*
      ii) Why are these compounds **not** harmful to the environment?   *(1 mark)*
   d) Suggest why pollution from cars is less when using ethanol instead of petrol.   *(1 mark)*

   e) Give **one** reason why ethanol is **not** used as a fuel for cars in Britain.   *(1 mark)*
   f) Some information about octane and ethanol is shown.

Property	Octane	Ethanol
Melting point in °C	−57	−113
Boiling point in °C	125	78.5
Density in g/cm^3	0.70	0.79
Heat produced in kJ/mol	5512	1367

Explain a similarity between octane and ethanol that allows ethanol to be used as a fuel in cars.
                                              (2 marks)

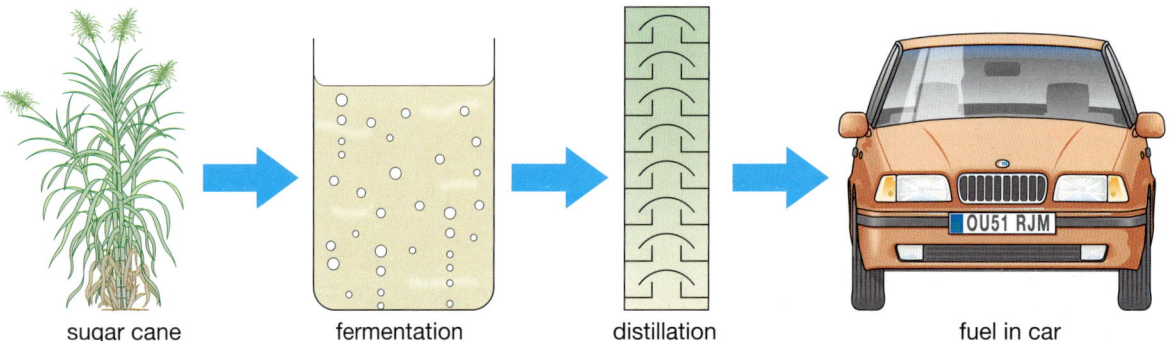

sugar cane   fermentation   distillation   fuel in car

2 a) Use words from the list to copy and complete the passage about organic compounds.

> carbon   carbon dioxide   electricity
> energy   fuels   neutral   non-renewable
> renewable   water   wood

Some organic compounds are used as _____ because they release energy when they are burned.
Some of these substances come from fossils.
Once used up they cannot be replaced.
This means they are _____.
All organic compounds contain the element _____. Many also contain the element hydrogen.
When organic compounds containing hydrogen are burned in plentiful supply of air, the two substances formed are _____ and water. *(4 marks)*

b) Why is it dangerous to burn organic compounds in a limited supply of air? *(2 marks)*

3 Petrol is a fuel used for cars. It is a mixture of hydrocarbons.

a) Name the **two** products formed when a hydrocarbon is burned completely in air. *(2 marks)*

b) i) Name the poisonous gas that is formed when a hydrocarbon is burned in a limited supply of air. *(1 mark)*

ii) Explain why this gas is poisonous. *(2 marks)*

c) Petrol is a fossil fuel and so its supply is limited. Alternative fuels will be needed as it runs out. The table shows data from 1998 for petrol and some alternative fuels.

Fuel	Cost of 100 g (pence)	Energy per 100 g (kJ)	Energy per penny (kJ)
petrol	6.8	4800	706
diesel oil	6.4	4700	734
ethanol	8.5	2900	341
hydrogen	20.0	14300	715
vegetable oil	9.0	3800	422

i) Use the data in the table to explain why diesel oil seems to be a good alternative to petrol. *(1 mark)*

ii) From your knowledge of fuels, give **one** disadvantage of using diesel oil as a replacement fuel for petrol. *(1 mark)*

iii) From the table, hydrogen seems to be a good alternative to petrol. Suggest **one** advantage and **two** disadvantages of using hydrogen as a fuel for cars. *(3 marks)*

4 The table shows some information about alkanes.

Name	Formula	Relative formula mass	Boiling point in °C
methane	CH_4	16	−160
ethane	C_2H_6	30	−90
propane		44	−40
butane	C_4H_{10}	58	
pentane	C_5H_{12}	72	36
hexane	C_6H_{14}	86	68

a) Give the formula of propane. *(1 mark)*

b) i) What happens to the boiling points of the alkanes as the relative formula mass increases? *(1 mark)*

ii) Draw a graph on a grid, with Relative formula mass on horizontal axis and Boiling point (°C) on vertical axis. Plot the points and draw a best fit line. *(3 marks)*

iii) What is the boiling point of butane? *(1 mark)*

iv) Show clearly on the graph how you found the boiling point of butane. *(1 mark)*

c) Which of the following is **not** an alkane.

C_7H_{16} C_9H_{18} $C_{11}H_{24}$ $C_{24}H_{50}$ *(1 mark)*

21

5 This question is about hydrocarbons.
The table below gives some information about the first ten members of an homologous series. It includes their melting points and boiling points. It was taken from a German Chemistry Textbook.

a) i) Name the homologous series. *(1 mark)*
   ii) What is meant by an *homologous series*? *(2 marks)*
   iii) Use the information in the table to predict the boiling point of C_9H_{20}. *(1 mark)*
   iv) What is the formula of the twelfth member of this series? *(1 mark)*

b) There are **three** hydrocarbons which have the molecular formula C_5H_{12}. The structural formula of one of these is shown opposite (A).

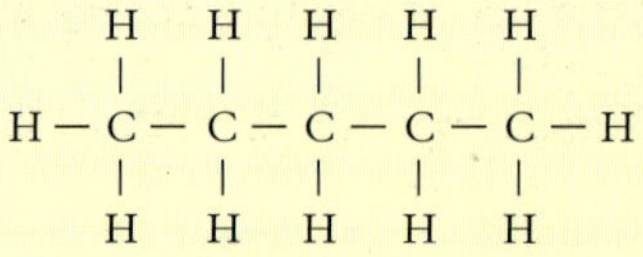

```
     H   H   H   H   H
     |   |   |   |   |
 H — C — C — C — C — C — H
     |   |   |   |   |
     H   H   H   H   H
```
(A)

i) Draw the structural formula of the other two compounds (B and C). *(2 marks)*
ii) What name is given to compounds which have the same molecular formula but different structures? *(1 mark)*
iii) Which of the compounds, A, B or C, has the highest boiling point? Give reasons for your answer. *(3 marks)*

Name	Summenformel	Strukturformelin (Kurzform)	Schmelztemperatur (°C)	Siedetemperatur (°C)
Methan	CH_4	CH_4	−182	−162
Äthan	C_2H_6	CH_3–CH_3	−183	−89
Propan	C_3H_8	CH_3–CH_2–CH_3	−188	−42
Butan	C_4H_{10}	CH_3–$(CH_2)_2$–CH_3	−138	0
Pentan	C_5H_{12}	CH_3–$(CH_2)_3$–CH_3	−130	+36
Hexan	C_6H_{14}	CH_3–$(CH_2)_4$–CH_3	−95	+69
Heptan	C_7H_{16}	CH_3–$(CH_2)_5$–CH_3	−90	+98
Octan	C_8H_{18}	CH_3–$(CH_2)_6$–CH_3	−57	+126
Nonan	C_9H_{20}	CH_3–$(CH_2)_7$–CH_3	−54	
Decan	$C_{10}H_{22}$	CH_3–$(CH_2)_8$–CH_3	−30	+174

Chapter 2

Industrial processes

2.1	
Co-ordinated	**Modular**
10.7	22 (15.1)

Sulphuric acid

Manufacture

Sulphuric acid is made from sulphur, air and water. These substances are relatively inexpensive so the process of manufacturing sulphuric acid is cost effective.

Did you know?

In America, sulphur deposits are found about 200 metres below the surface. Conventional mining would be difficult because the deposits are beneath quicksand. The sulphur is obtained by the Frasch process.

In this process, pressurised water at 155°C is pumped down a 15 cm diameter tube into the ground. The hot water melts the sulphur in the rock and forces it back up the pipe. Compressed air also helps force the sulphur to the surface. The hot water goes down the outside tube ensuring that the inside of the pipe keeps hot so the rising sulphur does not solidify in the pipe. Sulphur produced by this method is 99.5% pure.

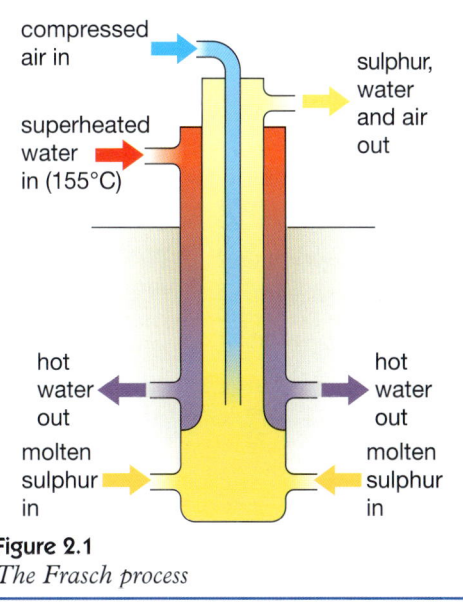

Figure 2.1
The Frasch process

23

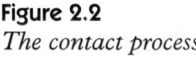

Did you know?

Cost is an important consideration in industrial processes. The capital outlay to build industrial chemical plants is huge. If the running costs are high, the product is comparatively expensive. This means that the invention of a cheaper method will make the original process too expensive and the large investment will be wasted. Processes that use cheap ingredients are unlikely to be undercut. This principle is used in the manufacture of ammonia (from air and water), nitric acid (from ammonia, air and water), sodium hydroxide, chlorine and hydrochloric acid (from sodium chloride and water) and sulphuric acid (from sulphur, air and water).

Usually industrial chemical plants do not produce much pollution. This is partly for economic reasons. Wasting materials costs money so as much as possible is recycled.

Most of the world's sulphuric acid is made by the **contact process**. The process is shown in Figure 2.2. In this process molten sulphur is burned in excess air. Sulphur dioxide (SO_2) is produced in the following reaction.

$$S + O_2 \rightarrow SO_2$$

The sulphur dioxide and any remaining air pass into a converter where more air is added and the sulphur dioxide is oxidised to sulphur trioxide (SO_3). This is a **reversible reaction**. The reaction requires a **catalyst** and vanadium oxide (V_2O_5) is required. A pressure of up to about 2 atmospheres is required.

$$2SO_2 + O_2 \rightleftharpoons 2SO_3$$

Figure 2.2
The contact process

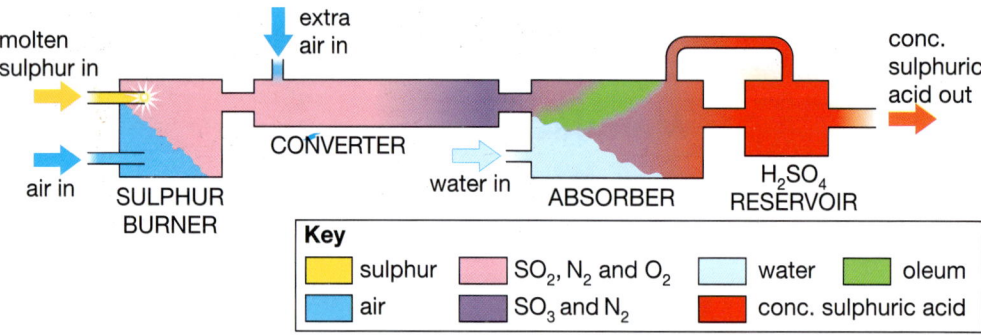

The process is strongly **exothermic**. This means that the maximum yield of sulphur trioxide should occur at low temperatures. Unfortunately, even with a catalyst, the reaction is too slow and temperatures of about 450°C are required. From the equation, three 'volumes' of reactants (two volumes of SO_2 and one volume of O_2) produce two volumes of product (SO_3), so increasing the pressure should produce more product. In fact the reaction goes almost to completion even at atmospheric pressure so high pressure (which means extra costs) is not used. The addition of extra air increases the amount of oxygen present. Excess oxygen increases the amount of product.

Figure 2.3
The contact process takes place in plants like this one in Billingham in Cleveland, UK

Theoretically the last stage of the manufacture is to react the sulphur trioxide with water.

$$SO_3 + H_2O \rightarrow H_2SO_4$$

However it is not possible to get sulphur trioxide to react directly with water. This is because the reaction is also very exothermic and produces a fine mist of concentrated acid, which is difficult to control. Instead the sulphur trioxide is dissolved in concentrated sulphuric acid to produce fuming sulphuric acid – sometimes called oleum. The fuming sulphuric acid is carefully diluted with water to produce concentrated sulphuric acid. The acid produced is about 98% pure; the remaining 2% is water.

This is another very exothermic process.

Uses of sulphuric acid

Sulphuric acid is the acid used in car batteries. It is also used in the manufacture of fertilisers and detergents (see Figure 2.4)

Figure 2.4
All these products were made using sulphuric acid as a raw material

Sulphuric acid as a dehydrating agent

A **dehydrating agent** is a substance that will remove water. Concentrated sulphuric acid is a powerful dehydrating agent. It is so powerful that it will even remove the elements of water from a compound.

If concentrated sulphuric acid is added to sugar, the sugar is dehydrated and carbon is produced. This reaction is shown in Figure 2.5.

$$C_{12}H_{22}O_{11} \xrightarrow{\text{conc. } H_2SO_4} 12C + 11H_2O$$

Concentrated sulphuric acid will also dehydrate copper(II) sulphate crystals by removing the **water of crystallisation**. When this happens the blue crystals turn white (see Figure 2.6).

Figure 2.5
The reaction between concentrated sulphuric acid and sugar

$$CuSO_4.5H_2O \xrightarrow{\text{conc. } H_2SO_4} CuSO_4 + 5H_2O$$

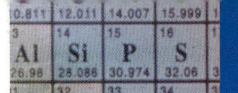

Figure 2.6
The reaction between concentrated sulphuric acid and copper(II) sulphate

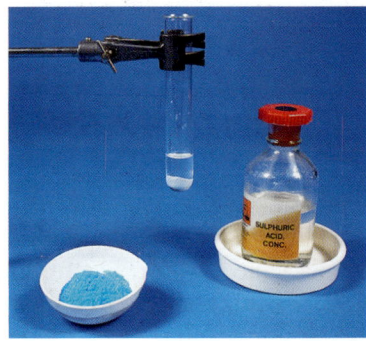

Topic questions

1 Name the raw materials used in the manufacture of sulphuric acid.

2 What is the name of the process used to manufacture sulphuric acid?

3 The manufacture of sulphuric acid uses a temperature of 450°C. What would be the advantages and disadvantages of using:
   a) 250°C   b) 650°C?

4 Give **three** uses for sulphuric acid.

5 Give an example of a reaction where concentrated sulphuric acid acts as a dehydrating agent.

Summary

◆ Sulphuric acid is made from the readily available, inexpensive materials sulphur, air and water.

◆ Sulphuric acid is made by the **contact process**.

◆ Sulphuric acid is used in the manufacture of car batteries, fertilisers and detergents.

◆ Sulphuric acid is a **dehydrating agent**. It will dehydrate carbohydrates like sugar to produce carbon. It will also dehydrate blue copper(II) sulphate crystals producing white anhydrous copper(II) sulphate.

2.2	
Co-ordinated	**Modular**
10.7	22 (15.2)

Aluminium

Aluminium is above iron in the reactivity series. This means that aluminium should corrode quite quickly. In fact aluminium is resistant to corrosion. When first exposed to air, the surface of the metal rapidly **oxidises** but the layer of aluminium oxide formed seals the surface and prevents any further attack. If the oxide layer is removed, the aluminium will react quite rapidly (see Figure 2.7).

Figure 2.7
When the oxide coating of aluminium has been removed, aluminium reacts rapidly with water

	0.811	12.011	14.007	15.999	1
	3	14	15	16	1
	Al	Si	P	S	
	26.98	28.086	30.974	32.06	3
	1	32	33	34	3

For some applications a thicker protective layer is needed. The process of **anodising** (Figure 2.8) can produce this thicker layer. In the anodising process the existing aluminium oxide layer is removed with sodium hydroxide solution. The aluminium object is then placed in dilute sulphuric acid and made into the **anode (positive electrode)**. Oxygen forms on the surface of the aluminium and a much thicker oxide layer is produced.

Figure 2.8
Aluminium is anodised to thicken its protective oxide coating

---

Did you know?

Aluminium oxide dissolves in sodium hydroxide because it behaves like an acidic oxide! This is very unusual as acidic oxides are usually non-metal oxides.

$$Al_2O_3 \; + \; 2NaOH \rightarrow 2NaAlO_2 \; + \; H_2O$$

The substance $NaAlO_2$ is called sodium aluminate.

Aluminium oxide will also behave like a basic oxide. It can be made to dissolve in some acids to produce aluminium salts.

Oxides that can behave as acids or bases depending on their environment are called amphoteric oxides.

	Li	Be	B	C	N	O	F	Ne
period 3	Na	Mg	Al	Si	P	S	Cl	Ar
	K	Ca						
nature of the oxide			?					

The diagram shows period 3 of the periodic table. On the left-hand side the oxides are very basic; on the right-hand side they are very acidic. Aluminium, in the middle, can be either acidic or basic depending on what it reacts with.

Summary

◆ Aluminium is relatively unreactive because of a protective oxide layer.

◆ The protective oxide layer on aluminium can be improved by **anodising**.

2.3	
Co-ordinated	Modular
10.7	22 (15.3)

Titanium

Uses of titanium

Titanium is a **transition metal**. It is strong, **corrosion resistant** and has quite a low **density**. This makes it ideal for the manufacture of aircraft. A titanium alloy was used to make the fuselage of Concorde.

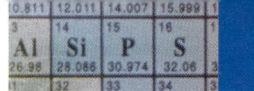

Figure 2.9
Titanium was used in the manufacture of Concorde

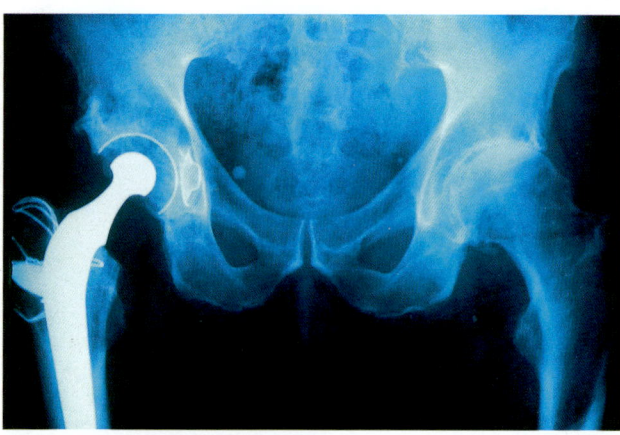

Figure 2.10
This hip joint is made of titanium

Titanium is also used to make replacement hip joints and in various parts of nuclear reactors.

Manufacture of titanium

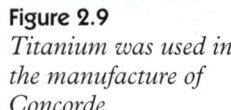

Did you know?

Titanium is the ninth most abundant element in the Earth's crust. It is about 10 times more abundant than copper.

Titanium is too high in the **reactivity series** to be prepared by **smelting** like iron.

Most reactive metals – like aluminium – are produced by **electrolysis**. Titanium cannot be manufactured this way because its ore is covalently bonded and does not conduct electricity. The common ore of titanium is **rutile** (titanium oxide). The oxide is converted into titanium(IV) chloride ($TiCl_4$) which is also covalently bonded. The titanium(IV) chloride is then reduced by heating it with a more reactive metal like sodium or magnesium.

$$4Na + TiCl_4 \rightarrow Ti + 4NaCl \quad \text{or} \quad 2Mg + TiCl_4 \rightarrow Ti + 2MgCl_2$$

The reaction, which is exothermic, is carried out in special, sealed furnaces (see Figure 2.11). The noble gas argon is put into the furnace to remove all traces of air. If air were present, the sodium or magnesium would react with the oxygen.

Figure 2.11
Titanium is produced in special sealed furnaces

Topic questions

1 Aluminium is above iron in the reactivity series. Explain why aluminium does not corrode as rapidly as iron.

2 What is the name of the process used to improve the protective layer on aluminium?

3 Explain why titanium cannot be produced by:
   a) smelting   b) electrolysis.

4 Why is argon used in the manufacture of titanium?

Summary

◆ Titanium is a low density, **corrosion resistant, transition metal.**

◆ Titanium is used to manufacture some aircraft. It is also used to make artificial hip joints.

◆ Titanium is produced by heating titanium(IV) chloride with a metal high in the **reactivity series** like sodium or magnesium.

2.4		Steel
Co-ordinated	Modular	
10.7	22 (15.2)	

The manufacture of pure iron and steel

Cast iron produced by a **blast furnace** is very impure. Among other substances it contains up to 4% carbon. The carbon makes the cast iron very brittle. For many applications cast iron is not suitable. For example, it would not be very sensible to make a hammer from a brittle material like cast iron!

Did you know?

The world's first cast iron bridge was erected at Ironbridge, Shropshire in 1779. It used 400 tonnes of cast iron. One hundred and ten years later, the Eiffel Tower was built in Paris. It used about 7000 tonnes of wrought iron. Wrought iron is better than cast iron but a suitable method of removing the carbon from the iron on a large scale was not available until Sir Henry Bessemer introduced a process in 1859.

To make pure iron, the carbon (and other impurities) have to be removed. This is done by pouring the molten iron from the blast furnace into a special furnace called a converter (Figures 2.12 and 2.13). Scrap iron is put in the converter first to reduce the damage to the furnace. If the scrap iron was not present, the thermal shock of the hot iron hitting the much cooler converter lining could crack the lining. (Rather like pouring boiling water into a milk bottle can cause the glass to break.)

Most of the impurities in iron are **non-metals**. In the furnace these are converted into non-metal oxides by passing pure oxygen through the molten iron.

These are examples of redox reactions.

Carbon is oxidised to carbon dioxide and comes off as a gas. Other non-metals (mainly silicon) also form oxides. These oxides are acidic and are removed by **neutralising** them with limestone (calcium carbonate). The product of this neutralisation is **slag** (mainly calcium silicate) which floats on top of the molten iron and can be removed.

Figure 2.12
Iron is converted to steel in an oxygen furnace

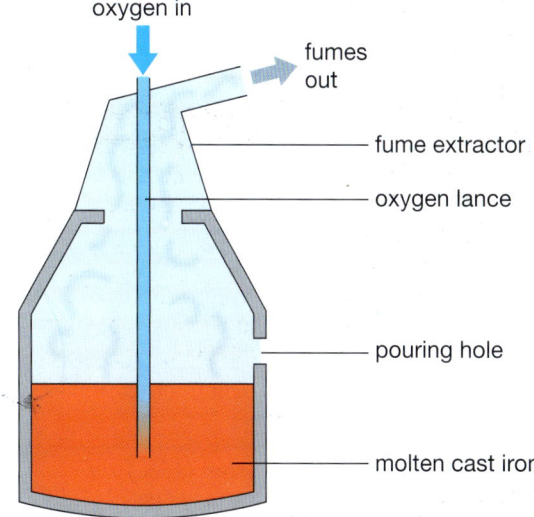

Figure 2.13
The inside of an oxygen converter where cast iron is purified

29

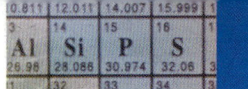

Pure iron is useful in some applications but most of the iron is made into **steel**. To do this, other elements have to be added to the iron. This can either be done by adding the element to the molten iron or adding scrap iron containing known amounts of other elements to the molten iron in the converter.

This process can produce between 400 and 500 tonnes of steel an hour.

Types of steel and their uses

Steel is an **alloy** of iron and carbon. There are many different sorts of steel. The properties of each type of steel depend on how much carbon is added (see Figure 2.14). High carbon steels are very hard and strong but are brittle; they are used where hard wear is required – for example ball bearings and roller bearings. Medium carbon **mild steel** can easily be pressed into shape so is used to make car body panels. **Wrought iron** is almost pure iron and is easily bent into shape so is used for decorative purposes like making iron gates (see Figure 2.15).

Figure 2.14
Alloys of iron and carbon

Carbon percentage	Name	A typical use
4–5	cast iron	car engine blocks
0.8–1.5	high carbon steel	ball bearings
0.3–0.8	medium carbon steel	railway lines
<0.3	mild steel	car bodies
very low	wrought iron	ornamental gates

Figure 2.15
*These objects are all made from different types of steel. a) These automotive ball pins are made from high carbon steel.
b) Car doors are made from mild steel.
c) Ornate gates are made from wrought iron*

The addition of other alloying elements also affects the properties of the steel (see Figure 2.16).

Figure 2.16
Steels containing other alloying metals

Alloying metal(s)	Name	A typical use
chromium (up to 5%)	chromium steel	ball bearings
cobalt (up to 10%)	cobalt steel	magnets
chromium (18%) nickel (8%)	stainless steel	cutlery
tungsten (18%) chromium (4%) vanadium (1%)	tool steel	cutting tools for metal working lathes

Electroplating

Like most metals, iron and steel can be **electroplated**. In this process the steel object is completely covered in a thin layer of another metal. The steel object must be free of grease and corrosion. If the plating electrolyte and conditions are correctly controlled, the layer will stick firmly to the steel.

The objects to be electroplated are supported on a suitable jig. The jig and objects are put in the plating **electrolyte** and connected to the negative side of a power supply. The anodes are connected to the positive side of the supply. The anodes are made of the pure metal that is to be plated onto the objects. The electrolyte contains ions of that metal (see Figures 2.17 and 2.18)

The electrode reactions are:

At the anode:

$$M(s) \rightarrow M^{n+}(aq) + ne^-$$

For example with silver plating:

$$Ag(s) \rightarrow Ag^+(aq) + e^-$$

At the **cathode**:

$$M^{n+}(aq) + ne^- \rightarrow M(s)$$

For example with silver plating:

$$Ag^+(aq) + e^- \rightarrow Ag(s)$$

Figure 2.17
An electroplating bath in operation

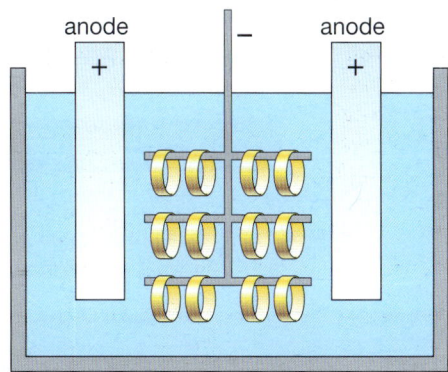

Figure 2.18
Electroplating

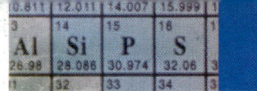

Figure 2.19
These items of cutlery have all been electroplated

Industrial processes

For every atom of metal that changes into an ion at the anode, one ion changes back to the metal at the cathode. This means that the concentration of the electrolyte doesn't change. All that happens is the anodes gradually 'dissolve' in the **electrolyte**.

Electroplating is used either to protect steel from corrosion or to produce a decorative finish to a product. Steel objects electroplated with silver look like silver objects but are very much cheaper.

Almost any metal can be plated on to the steel object. Silver, gold, nickel and chromium are frequently used.

Electroplating is an example of a **redox reaction**.

At the anode, the metal is oxidised to a positive ion (loss of electrons) and at the cathode, the ions are reduced back to the metal (gain of electrons).

The anode is positively charged because it is deficient in electrons. It works like an oxidising agent by accepting electrons from the metal. The negatively-charged cathode has an excess of electrons. It behaves like a reducing agent by providing electrons to the metal ions in the electrolyte.

Did you know?

Because electroplating is done in aqueous solutions, only metals below hydrogen in the reactivity series can be plated onto steel. This is not a problem as electroplating is usually used to reduce the risk of corrosion – so reactive metals would not be suitable.

If a steel object is placed in a bath of silver electrolyte, a chemical reaction takes place before the electric current can be switched on:

$$Fe(s) + 2Ag^+(aq) \rightarrow 2Ag(s) + Fe^{2+}(aq)$$

This happens because iron is more reactive than silver. Although only a very small amount of silver is chemically deposited on the steel, it weakens the adhesion between the electroplated silver and the steel. This means the plating is more likely to flake off.

For the highest quality work this is overcome by using several electroplating baths. The first bath would be a very dilute nickel electrolyte to 'flash' plate with a very thin layer of nickel. Because nickel is only slightly lower than iron in the reactivity series, there will be no chemical deposition. The process is repeated with a dilute copper electrolyte then a dilute silver electrolyte to 'flash' plate with each of these metals. Finally the object can be plated in a correct silver plating electrolyte.

Topic questions

1   What is the main difference between cast iron, wrought iron and steel?

2   In the basic oxygen converter to make steel, oxygen gas and calcium carbonate are added to the molten steel. What do each of these substances do?

3   What effect does a high chromium content have on the behaviour of steel?

4   Explain why the concentration of silver ions in a silver plating electrolyte does not change during the silver plating process.

Summary

- **Steel** is an **alloy** of iron and carbon.

- Steel is made from **cast iron** by the basic oxygen process.

- Alloying elements like tungsten and chromium can alter the properties of steel, making it harder or more corrosion resistant.

- **Electroplating** is a process in which metal objects are covered by a thin layer of another metal. The process can be used to protect steel against corrosion.

- Electroplating is a redox reaction.

Examination questions

1. The manufacture of sulphuric acid, H_2SO_4, by the Contact Process is shown below.

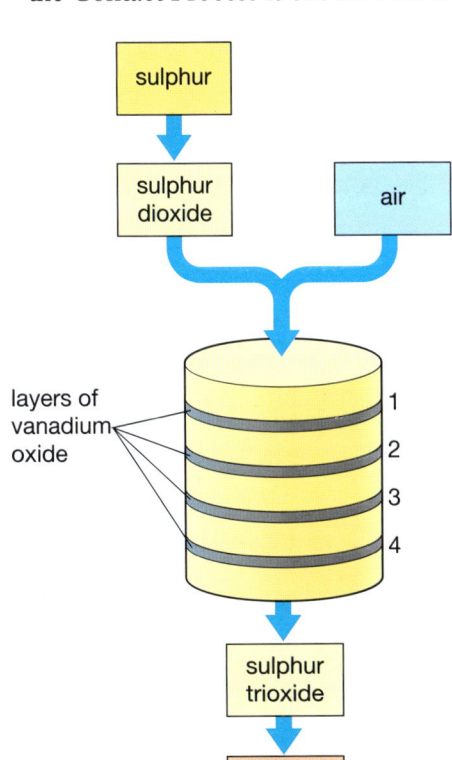

Vanadium oxide layer	Temperature of gas		% SO$_2$ changed into SO$_3$
	Before reaction	After reaction	
1	430	590	65
2	440	510	84
3	440	480	92
4	415	440	99

a) i) Name **one** source of sulphur. *(1 mark)*

   ii) How is sulphur dioxide made from sulphur? *(2 marks)*

b) i) What is the function of the vanadium oxide? *(1 mark)*

   ii) Use the information in the table to suggest why four layers of vanadium oxide are used. *(2 marks)*

   iii) What do the differences in temperature before and after each layer show about the reaction to make sulphur trioxide? *(1 mark)*

   iv) Suggest what should happen to the 1% of sulphur dioxide that is **not** changed into sulphur trioxide. *(1 mark)*

c) How is sulphuric acid made from sulphur trioxide? *(2 marks)*

d) Work out the mass of sulphuric acid, H_2SO_4, that can be made from 4 tonnes of sulphur. Relative atomic masses H 1; O 16; S 32. *(2 marks)*

2 a) Sulphuric acid is produced in the United Kingdom from sulphur. The three main reactions for the production of sulphuric acid are represented by the equations below.

$$S + O_2 \rightarrow SO_2$$
$$2SO_2 + O_2 \rightarrow 2SO_3$$
$$SO_3 + H_2O \rightarrow H_2SO_4$$

Name **two** raw materials, other than sulphur, needed to make sulphuric acid. *(2 marks)*

b) Blue copper sulphate crystals can be used to show that sulphuric acid is concentrated.

 i) What colour change would you **see** when copper sulphate crystals are added to concentrated sulphuric acid? *(1 mark)*

 ii) Why does the colour of the crystals change? *(1 mark)*

c) A student diluted some concentrated sulphuric acid with water. The student thought the dilute acid was weak. The teacher said it was still a strong acid.
Why is the acid described as strong? *(1 mark)*

d) The teacher gave the student two solutions. One was a strong acid and the other a weak acid. The solutions were of the same concentration.
Describe a test the student could do to show which solution was the strong acid and which was the weak acid. Give the results of the test with both solutions.
(3 marks)

3 a) Describe how steel is manufactured using molten iron obtained from the blast furnace.
Your answer should include:
● the types of reaction occurring;
● the details of the conditions used;
● energy changes involved. *(5 marks)*

b) Suggest **two** factors which influence the location of plants associated with the manufacture of steel. *(2 marks)*

c) Give **two** reasons why it is important to recycle steel. *(2 marks)*

4 a) The table gives some information about steels. Complete the table by choosing properties from the list.
● soft and easily shaped
● strong but brittle
● resistant to corrosion
● rusts easily

Type of steel	Percentage (%) of carbon	Other elements present	Properties	
			strength	corrosion
high carbon	0.5–1.4		....	rusts quite easily
low carbon	0.04–1.15		....	....
stainless	0.05–1.10	Cr, Ni	strong and hard	....

(2 marks)

b) Steels are made from molten iron in a furnace. The diagram shows the substances which are added to the molten iron during steelmaking.

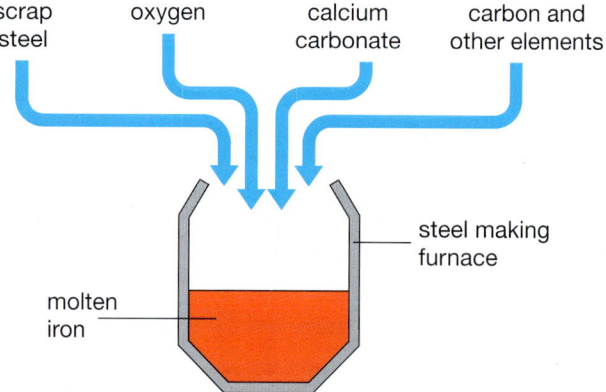

Give a reason why each of the substances is added to the molten iron. *(4 marks)*

c) i) Car bodies made of steel are painted. Explain how this prevents rusting. *(2 marks)*

 ii) The steel may be coated with zinc before it is painted. This gives further protection from rusting. Explain how this method of rust prevention works. *(2 marks)*

Chapter 3
Aqueous chemistry

3.1 Water is essential to life

Co-ordinated	Modular
10.15	21 (14.1)

Water is the most abundant substance on the Earth's surface. In fact nearly 71% of the Earth's surface is water.

Living things cannot survive without water. About 70% of body tissue is water. In some plant materials the water content can be over 90%. Each person needs to drink about 1.5 litres of water each day to replace what is lost in urine, faeces and sweat. In very hot weather this might go up to as much as 5 litres per day.

Purifying drinking water

Drinking water has to be treated to make it safe. Solids are removed in large filter beds then chlorine is added to kill any bacteria present. Other treatments may also be used depending on the purity of the water source (see Figure 3.1).

Did you know?

The total amount of water on the Earth's surface is about 1 370 000 000 cubic kilometres (1.37 × 10^9 km³). That's enough water to fill a garden hosepipe 1.4 million light years long.

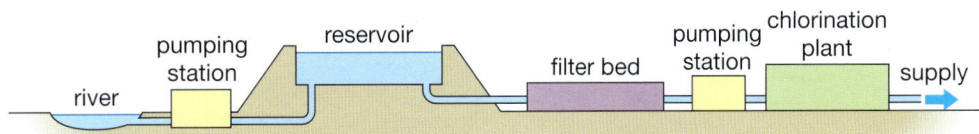

Figure 3.1
(a) The stages in a water treatment plant

This purification process does not remove all impurities. For example nitrates are not removed. Ammonium and nitrate ions can get into the water from the use of **artificial fertilisers**. Rain will wash the ammonium and nitrate ions into the ground. Normally the roots of the plant would remove these ions and use them for growth, but if fertilisers are over used (or if rainfall is very heavy) some of the ions can be washed past the root systems before the roots can absorb them. These ions then drain into streams and can get into drinking water. The water companies carefully monitor the nitrate content of drinking water as too much is harmful, especially to bottle-fed babies.

Figure 3.1
(b) This water treatment plant is in British Columbia in Canada

Did you know?

Nitrates in water are turned into nitrites in the intestine. They can re-enter the body and react to form carcinogenic (cancer-forming) compounds called nitrosamines.

In babies the nitrites can interfere with haemoglobin, limiting its ability to carry oxygen. The baby develops a fatal form of anaemia called 'blue-baby syndrome'. There have been no deaths from this recorded in the UK since 1948.

It is possible to remove nitrates from domestic drinking water by ion exchange (see section 3.3) or reverse osmosis equipment, but these are fairly expensive. Increasing numbers of people drink bottled water to reduce their intake of potentially harmful substances in water. But bottled water often has a much higher level of bacteria than tap water.

Summary

◆ Water is essential to life.

3.2	
Co-ordinated	Modular
10.15	21 (14.1)

The water cycle

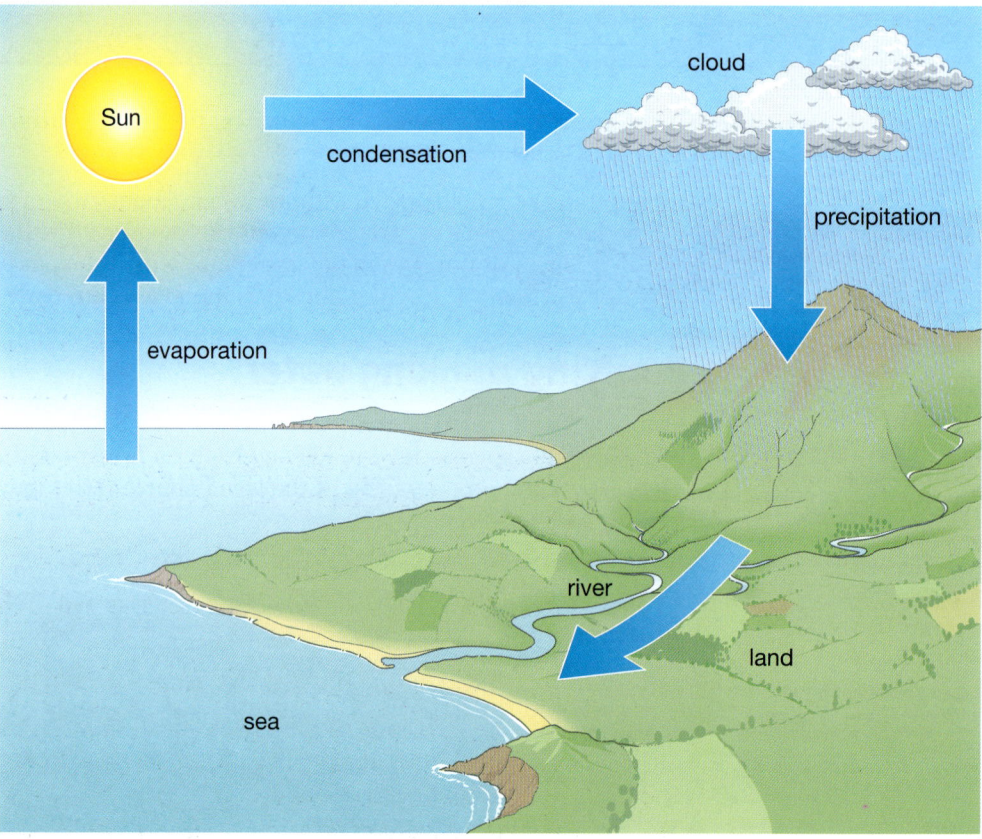

Figure 3.2
The water cycle

Water in rivers, lakes and seas is evaporated by the heat of the Sun. The pure water vapour rises and cools. As it cools, the water vapour condenses to form clouds. As the clouds cool further, rain, and other forms of precipitation like snow and hail, are produced. This process is called the **water cycle**.

The rain that falls starts off as fairly pure water. As it falls it will dissolve some carbon dioxide from the air. Once it gets into the ground it will dissolve a lot more carbon dioxide. It may also dissolve other substances from the soil. The water can also dissolve substances from the rocks as it passes through them.

One of the substances dissolved by the water as it passes through the rock is sodium chloride (common salt). The water will not have much salt in it as it flows down river but over many millions of years, the amount has built up in the sea so that seawater now contains quite a high salt content.

Figure 3.3
The extraction of sea salt from sea water

Did you know?

Seawater contains about 3% sodium chloride. It also contains many other substances.

Magnesium   0.13%
Calcium   0.04%
Potassium   0.04%
Bromine   0.006%

There is gold in seawater. The percentage is very low (about $6 \times 10^{-10}\%$), but the total amount of gold in all the oceans in the world is about 8 million tonnes. It would, however, cost more to get the gold out of the water than it would be worth.

Summary

◆ The **water cycle** is the process in which water, **evaporated** from the sea by the heat of the Sun, falls back to Earth by **precipitation** and eventually flows back to the sea.

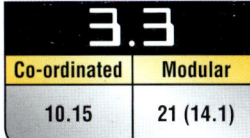

3.3	
Co-ordinated	Modular
10.15	21 (14.1)

Hard and soft water

The reaction between rainwater and limestone

Rainwater containing carbon dioxide can react with limestone in the following reaction.

$$CaCO_3(s) + H_2O(l) + CO_2(aq) \rightarrow Ca(HCO_3)_2(aq)$$

The limestone (calcium carbonate, $CaCO_3(s)$) is not soluble in water but it reacts with the water and carbon dioxide to produce calcium hydrogencarbonate ($Ca(HCO_3)_2(aq)$) which *is* soluble in water. Over thousands of years this process has gradually made huge potholes and caverns in the limestone rocks.

37

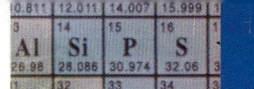

Figure 3.4
This cave formed when the limestone dissolved in the acidic rain water

This reaction is reversible. Once the very dilute calcium hydrogencarbonate solution gets into the open cavern, some of the carbon dioxide in the water is given off. This causes the reaction to go in the other direction.

$$Ca(HCO_3)_2(aq) \rightarrow CaCO_3(s) + H_2O(l) + CO_2(g)$$

The limestone forms where the water emerges from cracks in the rock. This causes stalagmites and stalactites to form.

> **Did you know?**
>
> The reason why there is not a large amount of calcium hydrogencarbonate in the oceans is because it decomposes in the warm seas to form calcium carbonate solid which is deposited as layers and eventually forms rock. Sea creatures also remove the calcium to form their shells of calcium carbonate.

The cause of hard and soft water

Water containing dissolved calcium ions (Ca^{2+}) is called **hard water**. If drinking water is extracted from rivers that have their source in limestone areas, the water will contain calcium hydrogencarbonate and will be hard. There is another substance that can make water hard. That substance is calcium sulphate. Calcium sulphate is found in the rocks gypsum and alabaster and is slightly soluble in water. Rocks containing magnesium behave in a similar way and the magnesium ion (Mg^{2+}) can also make water hard.

Hardness caused by calcium hydrogencarbonate is called **temporary hardness** because it can easily be removed by heating the water

$$Ca(HCO_3)_2(aq) \rightarrow CaCO_3(s) + H_2O(l) + CO_2(g)$$

Hardness caused by calcium sulphate cannot be removed by heating and is called **permanent hardness**.

Water containing no calcium or magnesium ions is called **soft water**.

The effects of hard water

a) Good effects

The substances dissolved in hard water are good for your health. Calcium ions are needed to build healthy teeth and bones. There is also evidence that calcium ions help to reduce the incidence of heart disease.

0.811	12.011	14.007	15.999	
3	14	15	16	
Al	**Si**	**P**	**S**	
26.98	28.086	30.974	32.06	3
	32	33	34	3

b) Bad effects

1 **Soaps** are compounds that help to remove oily material from clothes. They are the sodium salts of carboxylic acids (see Chapter 1). In soaps the carboxylic acids contain long chains of carbon atoms. Sodium soaps are soluble in water. If the water contains calcium ions, the following reaction occurs between the soap and the calcium ions.

sodium 'soap' + calcium ions → calcium 'soap' + sodium ions
(soluble)   (insoluble 'scum')

The calcium soap is not soluble in water. It forms a greasy '**scum**' that sticks to clothes. The reaction stops the soap from working so a lot of extra soap is required to produce lather. This makes the washing process much more expensive.

2 Hard water can also cause a build up a deposit of '**limescale**' in kettles and boilers. If the hardness is caused by calcium hydrogencarbonate, the scale is a deposit of calcium carbonate formed by the reverse of the reaction that put the hardness in the water.

$$Ca(HCO_3)_2(aq) \rightarrow CaCO_3(s) + H_2O(l) + CO_2(aq)$$
limescale

The deposit reduces the efficiency of the kettle or boiler because it is not a good conductor of heat. This increases the cost of producing hot water. Scale can also accumulate in boilers and may eventually damage the boiler.

Removing hardness

To remove hardness, the dissolved calcium and magnesium ions have to be removed. There are several ways of doing this.

1 Precipitating the calcium and magnesium ions

The addition of sodium carbonate will remove the calcium and magnesium ions. As the sodium carbonate dissolves in the hard water, the carbonate ions react with the calcium ions to produce calcium carbonate which is not soluble in water. Calcium carbonate forms as a precipitate.

$$Na_2CO_3(aq) + Ca(HCO_3)_2(aq) \rightarrow 2NaHCO_3(aq) + CaCO_3(s)$$

Washing 'soda' and bath salts contain sodium carbonate and this is how they work to soften water.

2 Using ion exchange to remove calcium and magnesium ions

Ion exchange columns contain a porous material that has a lot of negatively-charged sites on it. Attached to these sites are positive ions, usually sodium ions (Na^+) or hydrogen ions (H^+). When water containing calcium or magnesium ions passes down the column, these ions displace the sodium or hydrogen ions. The material holds the calcium or magnesium ions so the water that comes from the bottom of the tube has no calcium or magnesium ions in it. This is now soft water.

After a while the material in the column has to be renewed. This is done by reversing the process and washing out the calcium ions with a concentrated solution of sodium ions (using salt solution) or hydrogen ions (using an acid like hydrochloric acid).

Figure 3.5
The scum around this bath has been formed because of the calcium salts in the water

Figure 3.6
You can see how limescale has built up in this domestic metal pipe

Did you know?

Soapless detergents are not affected by hard water. This is because both the sodium and the calcium form of the detergent are soluble in water so no scum forms and the detergent works normally.

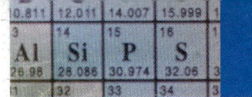

Figure 3.7
What happens in an ion exchange column

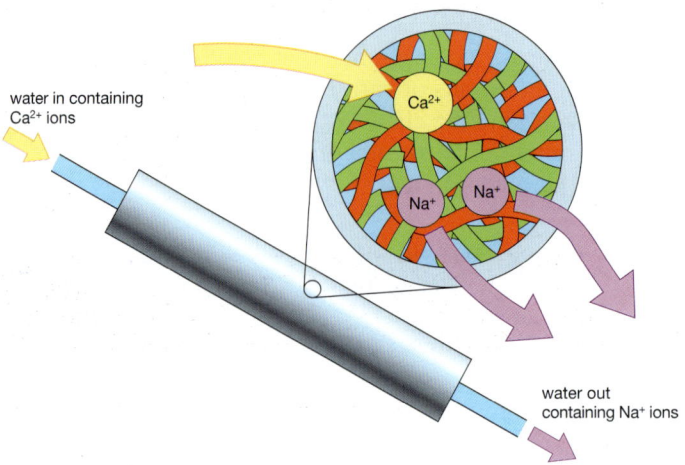

water in containing Ca²⁺ ions

water out containing Na⁺ ions

Topic questions

1 There are two main processes used in the purification of drinking water. How does each of these processes make the water pure?

2 Explain how nitrates can get into drinking water.

3 Outline the water cycle using the terms *evaporation*, *condensation* and *precipitation*.

4 Which **two** ions are mainly responsible for hard water?

5 a) Which substance in hard water can be removed by heating the water?
  b) What name is given to hardness that can be removed by heating water?

6 Explain how hardness can be removed by:

  a) washing 'soda'   b) ion exchange.

Summary

◆ **Hard water** contains calcium and/or magnesium ions.

◆ Hard water causes '**scum**' with soap and harmful '**limescale**' in kettles and boilers.

◆ Soft water contains few or no calcium and/or magnesium ions.

◆ Hard water can be **softened** by removing the calcium and/or magnesium ions either by **precipitation** or by **ion exchange**.

3.4	
Co-ordinated	Modular
10.15	21 (14.2)

Solubility

Water is a powerful **solvent**. Many substances are **soluble** in water. The ability of water to dissolve substances is widely used in industry. For example, in the metal plating industry (see Chapter 2) water is the solvent used for the electrolyte. In industry cost is important and water is a very cheap solvent. But not only is it cheap, for many applications water is also the best solvent. Water also has a high thermal capacity. This means it is very effective as a coolant. Water is still used as a coolant in many industrial processes (e.g. power stations) and in the engines of many motor vehicles. It is the coolant properties of water that enable it to be used effectively to put out fires.

The solubility of gases

Many gases are soluble in water. But water will not dissolve an infinite amount of gas – there is a maximum. The maximum amount of gas that will dissolve in water is called the **solubility**.

Figure 3.8 shows the solubilities of some gases in water. The figures show the maximum number of millilitres of gas that will dissolve in 1 millilitre of water. It is clear that there is a huge range in solubility. Nitrogen and oxygen are only slightly soluble but ammonia is very soluble. The table also shows that gases are more soluble in cold water than in hot water. This is why a glass of cold water left on a bedside table usually has small gas bubbles in it in the morning. Overnight the water warms up and the gases dissolved in it become less soluble (see Figure 3.9).

Figure 3.8
The solubility of some gases in water

Gas	Solubility in water (ml/ml)	
	0°C	60°C
nitrogen	0.024	0.01
oxygen	0.049	0.019
carbon dioxide	1.71	0.36
chlorine	4.61	1.01
hydrogen chloride	507	339
ammonia	1299	about 230

Figure 3.9
Bubbles have developed in the glass of water overnight

Figure 3.10
The bubbles rise when a bottle of fizzy drink is opened

Gases are also more soluble in water if the pressure is increased. This is why fizzy drinks always bubble when the top is opened (see Figure 3.10).

Carbon dioxide

Fizzy drinks are made using carbonated water – that is water with carbon dioxide dissolved in it under pressure. Carbon dioxide is used because it is readily available, cheap and non-toxic. It is better than oxygen or nitrogen because it is about 30 times more soluble and so makes the drinks fizzier.

Oxygen

Although oxygen is not very soluble in water, the amount that does dissolve is important to aquatic life. Fish and other animals extract the oxygen they need for **respiration** directly from the water. If the water is too hot then they will die because less oxygen is available in the water. This is why power stations have to be very careful to ensure that the cooling water they discharge into rivers and lakes is not too hot. The huge cooling towers at power stations are for this purpose.

Did you know?

Sparkling wines like champagne are also fizzy because of dissolved carbon dioxide. But in wines, the gas is not added, it is produced naturally in the wine during the fermentation process.

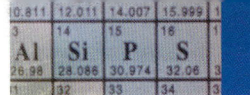

Figure 3.11
The cooling towers at a power station

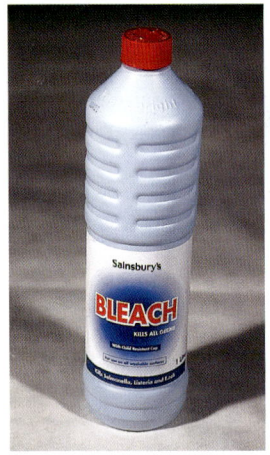

Figure 3.12
Household bleach contains chlorine water

Did you know?

If oxygen was more soluble in water then the oceans could dissolve more and there would be less oxygen in the atmosphere. At the average temperature of the oceans, 1 millilitre of water will dissolve 0.04 millilitres of oxygen. If the solubility of oxygen were doubled then the oxygen content of the atmosphere would drop from 21% to about 14%.

Chlorine

Chlorine is fairly soluble in water (see Figure 3.8). A solution of chlorine in water is called 'chlorine water'. It is used to bleach materials and to kill bacteria. Most domestic bleaches and some toilet cleaners contain chlorine water. Chlorine is also dissolved in the water of public swimming pools to reduce the risk of diseases being spread.

Figure 3.13
A chlorination plant at a swimming pool

The solubility of solids

Most **ionic compounds** are soluble in water, though some, for example calcium carbonate, are not. **Covalent compounds** are usually not soluble in water, though here too, there are exceptions, for example sugar.

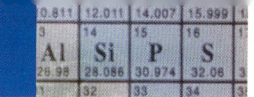

When a solid dissolves in water it forms a solution. Water is the **solvent** and the solid is the **solute**. The same principle applies to solids as to gases – there is a maximum amount of solute that will dissolve in a solvent. This maximum quantity is called the solubility. It is measured as the number of grams of solute that will dissolve in 100 grams of solvent. The solubility of solids depends on the temperature. Unlike gases, solids are usually more soluble in hot solvents. So when quoting the solubility of a substance it always necessary to specify the temperature.

A solution that has got the maximum possible amount of solute in it is called a **saturated solution**. If a saturated solution is cooled, less of the solute will be able to dissolve. The excess solute will separate from the solution as a solid – often in the form of crystals.

Figure 3.14
Table of the solubility of some solids at different temperatures

Substance	Temperature/°C						
	0	10	20	40	60	80	100
potassium nitrate	13.3	20.9	31.6	63.9	110	169	246
sodium chloride	35.7	35.8	36	36.6	37.3	38.4	39.8
potassium chloride	28.1	31.2	34.2	40	45.8	51.3	56.3
calcium hydroxide	0.185	0.176	0.165	0.141	0.116	0.094	0.077
copper(II) sulphate	14.3	17.4	20.7	28.5	40	55	75.4

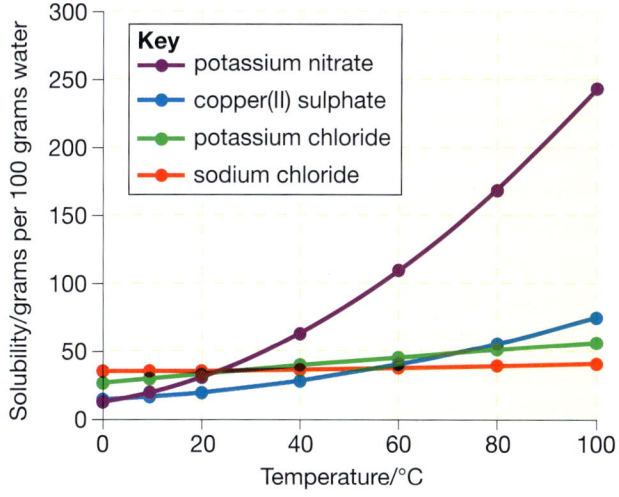

Figure 3.15
Solubilities of some common substances

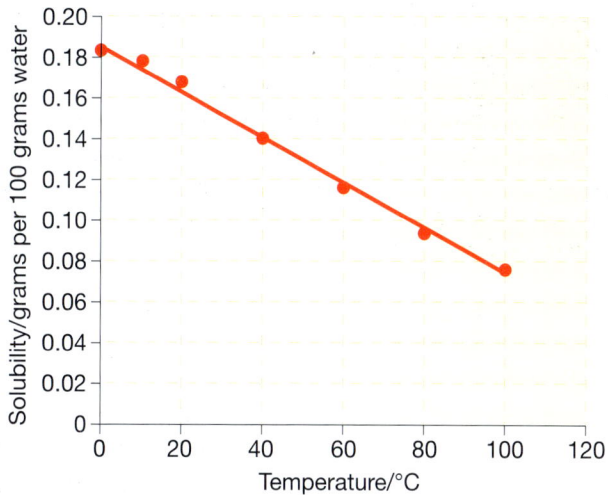

Figure 3.16
Solubility of calcium hydroxide

With solubilities there is a wide range of behaviour patterns. Some have quite low solubility at 0°C but very high solubility at 100°C (for example potassium nitrate), for others the solubility does not change much with the temperature (for example sodium chloride) and some have very low solubility (for example calcium hydroxide.) Calcium hydroxide shows another unusual pattern. Its solubility decreases as the temperature goes up.

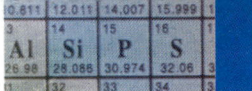

Using a solubility curve

Example 1

A saturated solution of potassium nitrate is made by dissolving the solute in 100 grams of water at 90°C. The solution is then cooled to room temperature (20°C). What mass of potassium nitrate crystals would be produced?

From the graph of the solubility of potassium nitrate:

Amount of potassium nitrate soluble in 100 g water at 90°C	205 g
Amount of potassium nitrate soluble in 100 g water at 20°C	32 g

When a saturated solution of potassium nitrate at 90°C is cooled to 20°C, then 205 − 32 = **173 g** of solid potassium nitrate are produced.

Example 2

A solution of copper(II) sulphate solution is boiled to remove some of the water. When the volume has been reduced to 500 ml, the solution is left to cool. At 80°C crystals of copper(II) sulphate begin to form. What mass of copper(II) sulphate will be formed when the solution has cooled to 20°C?

The solution becomes saturated at 80°C (when the crystals first begin to form).

From the graph, at 80°C 100 g of water will dissolve 55.0 grams of copper(II) sulphate.

100 g of water have a volume of about 100 ml, so 500 ml of copper sulphate solution will contain about 500 g of water.

If 100 g of water contain 55.0 g of copper(II) sulphate, then 500 g will contain about 5 × 55 = 275 g of copper(II) sulphate.

At 20°C 100 g of water will dissolve about 21 g of copper(II) sulphate.

So 500 g of water will contain about 5 × 21 = 105 g of copper(II) sulphate.

At 80°C there were 275 g of copper(II) sulphate dissolved in the water and at 20°C there were 105 g still dissolved in the water.

This means that the mass of the crystals produced must be 275 − 105 = **170 grams.**

Topic questions

1   What is meant by the words:

   a) solute?
   b) solvent?
   c) solution?

Al	Si	P	S
26.98	28.086	30.974	32.06

2 Complete the following sentences using the words in the box.

    less   more

    Most gases are _____ soluble in hot water than in cold water.

    Solids are usually _____ soluble in hot water.

3 What is the definition of solubility?

4 The table shows the solubility of ammonium chloride at different temperatures.

    a) Draw a graph of the solubility of ammonium chloride against temperature.
    b) What is the solubility of ammonium chloride at 25°C?
    c) What is the solubility of ammonium chloride at 75°C?
    d) How much ammonium chloride will crystallise from 200 ml of solution that is saturated at 75°C when it is cooled to room temperature of 25°C?

5 Air in the atmosphere contains about 20% oxygen. Explain why air dissolved in water contains about 33% oxygen.

Temp /°C	Solubility /g per 100 g
0	29.4
10	33.3
20	37.2
40	45.8
60	55.2
80	65.6
100	77.3

Summary

◆ The **solubility** of a substance at a particular temperature is the maximum number of grams of solute that will dissolve in 100 grams of solvent at that temperature.

◆ Gases are less soluble in hot water than in cold water.

◆ Solids are usually more soluble in hot water than in cold water.

3.5   Acids and bases

Co-ordinated	Modular
10.15	21 (14.3)

What is an acid?

The Arrhenius idea of an acid

Arrhenius was a Swedish scientist. In 1887 he put forward his theory of ionisation. The theory suggested that many substances in solution were dissociated into ions. His idea was not popular. Other scientists argued that it was not possible for a substance to break down in this way because of the amount of energy it required. For example when sodium reacts with chlorine to produce sodium chloride, a lot of energy is released. The scientists thought it was impossible that water could provide enough energy to reverse this change. Arrhenius pointed out that sodium ions and chloride ions were not the same as atoms and that the amount of energy required to separate ions was much less.

Figure 3.17
Arrhenius

Arrhenius extended his idea to acids and bases. He defined an **acid** as 'a substance which on dissolving in water dissociates to produce hydrogen ions'.

45

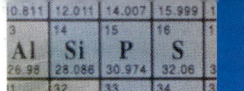

Did you know?

Most non-metal oxides are acidic even though the non-metal itself is not acidic. This is why early scientists thought that acidity was caused by oxygen. In fact the name 'oxygen' means 'acid creator'.

Figure 3.18
How a hydrogen atom becomes a hydrogen ion

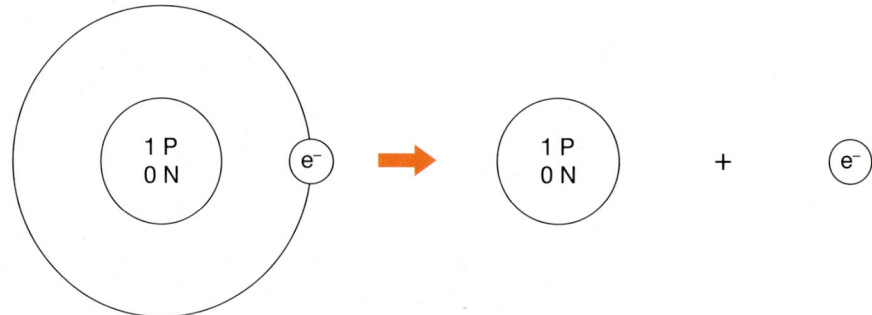

Figure 3.18 shows how a hydrogen atom can separate into a hydrogen ion and an **electron**. The hydrogen ion is just the **nucleus** of the hydrogen atom and contains only one proton. So a hydrogen ion is just a **proton**.

Hydrogen chloride is a gas. It is very soluble in water (see Figure 3.8). When it dissolves in water it forms a very acidic solution called hydrochloric acid. Figure 3.19 shows the stages in this process.

Figure 3.19
How hydrogen chloride reacts with water to form hydrochloric acid

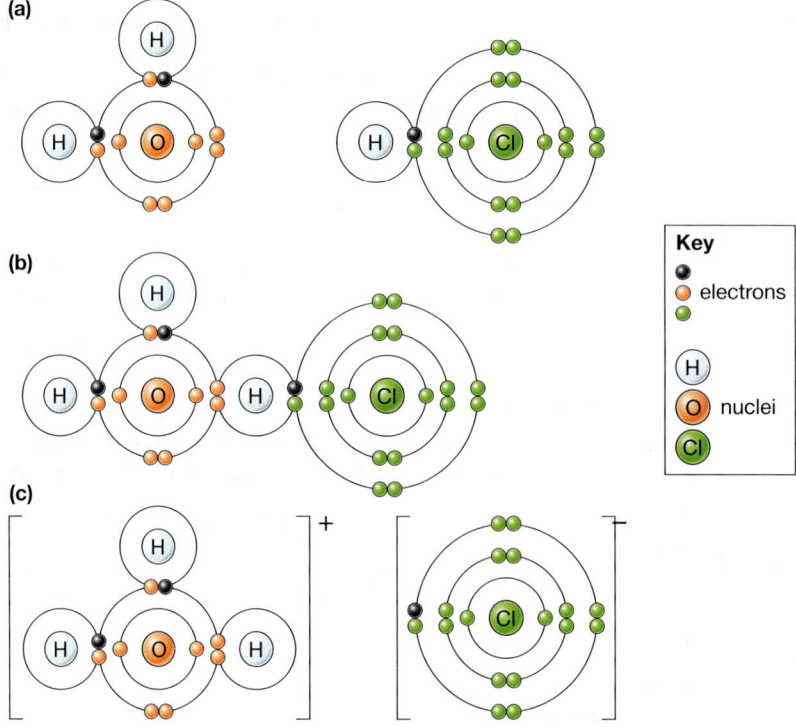

Figure 3.19 a) shows the covalent structures of hydrogen chloride and water. Because hydrogen chloride is covalently bonded, there are no hydrogen ions present so it is not acidic. When hydrogen chloride dissolves in water, a reaction takes place. In this reaction the hydrogen atom on the hydrogen chloride molecule attaches to one of the unused pairs of electrons (called 'lone pairs') on the oxygen atom in the water molecule. This breaks the bond between the hydrogen atom and the chlorine atom, as shown in Figure 3.19 c). The products are the H_3O^+ ion and the Cl^- ion. The H_3O^+ ion is just a **hydrated proton** (hydrogen ion) and is more usually written as $H^+(aq)$.

Hydrogen chloride is, therefore, not an acid until it dissolves in water.

Figure 3.20
(a) Blue litmus paper on concentrated sulphuric acid. (b) What happens when one drop of water is added to the litmus paper

Figure 3.20
(a) Blue litmus paper on concentrated sulphuric acid. (b) What happens when one drop of water is added to the litmus paper

The same is true of sulphuric acid. Concentrated sulphuric acid is not acidic. If a piece of blue litmus paper is placed on the surface of concentrated sulphuric acid, it remains blue (see Figure 3.20a). There are no hydrogen ions in concentrated sulphuric acid. But if one drop of water is added, the litmus paper turns red instantly (Figure 3.20b). When water is present the substance becomes acidic.

As a general rule, water must be present for a substance to act as an acid.

All the reactions that are typical of acids depend upon the acid having hydrated protons available (hydrogen ions). For this reason acids can be defined as **proton donors**.

What is a base?

The term '**base**' was first used in the 1770s by Rouelle to describe substances that react with acids to form salts. The familiar relationship is:

$$\text{base} + \text{acid} \rightarrow \text{salt} + \text{water}$$

Using this definition, a base is either a metal oxide or a metal hydroxide. The reaction between a base and an acid is called **neutralisation** because the 'power' of the acid is neutralised by the base. The key reaction that occurs is either:

$$2H^+(aq) + O^{2-} \rightarrow H_2O \quad \text{or} \quad H^+(aq) + OH^- \rightarrow H_2O$$

In each of these reactions the 'active ingredient' of the base uses a hydrated proton from the acid. So if acids are proton donors then bases can be defined as **proton acceptors**.

Alkalis

Most metal oxides and hydroxides are insoluble in water. Metal oxides that do dissolve in water react with it to form a hydroxide. This is illustrated by the reaction between calcium oxide (quicklime) and water to produce calcium hydroxide (slaked lime).

$$CaO(s) + H_2O(l) \rightarrow Ca(OH)_2(aq)$$

An **alkali** is a soluble base so all alkalis are metal hydroxides.

Arrhenius defined an alkali as 'a substance which on dissolving in water dissociates to produce OH^- ions.'

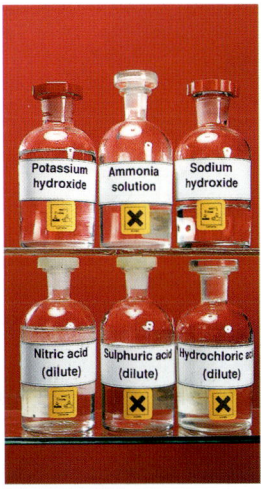

Figure 3.21
Some common acids and bases

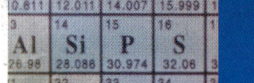

The Lowry and Brønsted theory of acids and bases

Figure 3.22
*a) Lowry and
b) Brønsted*

The Arrhenius idea of acids and bases is limited to the behaviour of substances when dissolved in water. The Lowry and Brønsted theory proposed in 1923 extends the Arrhenius idea to other situations.

Arrhenius defined an acid as 'a substance which on dissolving in water dissociates to produce hydrogen ions' and an alkali as 'a substance which on dissolving in water dissociates to produce hydroxide ions.' The Lowry and Brønsted theory defines an acid as 'a substance that can give up a proton to a base' and a base as 'any substance which can combine with a proton.' There is no reference to water in this definition.

Looking back at Figure 3.19, the Arrhenius definition of an acid would fit hydrogen chloride but nothing in the diagram would meet his definition of a base. Using the Lowry and Brønsted theory, hydrogen chloride still fits the definition of an acid but this time water fits the definition of a base because it combines with a proton.

The Arrhenius theory took a long time to be accepted because it was an entirely new idea that did not seem to fit with the scientific ideas of the time. But the Lowry and Brønsted theory was readily acceptable because it was a refinement of an existing idea (Arrhenius' idea) and because it also explained behaviours with non-aqueous solvents that the Arrhenius theory did not cover.

Strong and weak acids and bases

Strong and weak acids

Hydrogen chloride dissociates in water to form hydrochloric acid:

$$HCl + H_2O \rightarrow H_3O^+ + Cl^-$$

which can be simplified to:

$$HCl(aq) \rightarrow H^+(aq) + Cl^-(aq)$$

Ethanoic acid dissociates in the same way in the following reaction:

$$HOOC.CH_3(aq) \rightarrow H^+(aq) + {}^-OOC.CH_3(aq)$$

In hydrochloric acid almost all the hydrogen chloride dissociates into ions but in ethanoic acid, only about 0.3% of the acid is dissociated into ions.

Acids which are highly ionised are called **strong acids** while those which are only slightly ionised are called **weak acids**. By this definition, hydrochloric acid is a strong acid and ethanoic acid is a weak acid. Figure 3.23 summarises this idea.

Figure 3.23
The ionisation of strong and weak acids

$$HA(aq) \rightleftharpoons H^+(aq) + A^-(aq)$$
Ionisation of a strong acid

$$HA(aq) \rightleftharpoons H^+(aq) + A^-(aq)$$
Ionisation of a weak acid

Hydrochloric, sulphuric and nitric acids are examples of strong acids. Ethanoic, citric and carbonic acids are all examples of weak acids.

Strong and weak bases

Exactly the same idea applies to bases. **Strong bases**, like sodium and potassium hydroxides, are almost completely ionised in water but **weak bases**, like ammonia solution, are only slightly ionised.

The pH scale

A cubic decimetre of **molar** hydrochloric acid contains 1 **mole** of hydrogen chloride. Because the acid is 100% ionised, we can say that it contains 1 mole of hydrogen ions. The concentration of hydrogen ions is, therefore, 1 M (1 molar).

For the same volume of ethanoic acid of the same concentration, the number of moles of hydrogen ions is only about 0.003. In this case the concentration of hydrogen ions is 0.003 M (0.003 molar). In weaker acids or in more dilute solutions, the concentration of hydrogen ions is much lower.

Figure 3.24
The pH values of different acid concentrations

Concentration of hydrogen ions/mol dm^{-3}	pH
1×10^{-7}	7
1×10^{-6}	6
5×10^{-6}	5.3
1×10^{-4}	4
5×10^{-4}	4.3
0.001	3
0.005	2.3
0.01	2
0.05	1.3
0.1	1
0.5	0.3
1	0

The **pH scale** is a convenient way of representing very low concentrations of hydrogen ions. It runs from 0 to 14 and is defined as:

$$pH = -\log_{10}[\text{concentration of hydrogen ions}]$$

(Don't worry about the meaning of '$-\log_{10}$' – this is easily worked out with a calculator.)

The strongest acids have the lowest pH – around 0–1 on the scale. Strong alkalis have the highest pH – around 13–14. Neutral solutions have a pH of 7.

A molar solution of hydrochloric acid has a hydrogen ion concentration of 1 mol dm^{-3} so it has a pH of 0.

A molar solution of ethanoic acid has a hydrogen ion concentration of about 0.003 mol dm^{-3} so it has a pH of 2.52.

For the same concentration of acid, weak acids will have a higher pH.

Topic questions

1   a)   What is the Arrhenius definition of an acid?
    b)   Use this definition to explain why acids are called proton donors.

2   Explain why hydrogen chloride gas will not turn dry blue litmus paper red but will turn damp blue litmus paper red.

3   Complete the following general equation: acid + base → _____ + _____

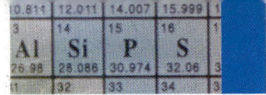
4   What is the difference between an alkali and a base?

5   When ammonia gas dissolves in water, a reaction takes place. The equation for the reaction is:

$$NH_3 + H_2O \rightleftharpoons NH_4^+ + OH^-$$

Use the Lowry and Brønsted theory to decide which of these substances are acids and which are bases.

6   What is the difference between a strong acid and a weak acid?

7   a) A solution of a strong base has a pH of 12. What would you expect the pH of a solution of a weak base of the same concentration to be?

A   7   C   12
B   between 7 and 12   D   greater than 12

b) Explain your answer to part a).

Summary

- **Acids** are substances that dissociate in water to produce hydrogen ions (Arrhenius).

- Substances like hydrogen chloride and concentrated sulphuric acid only behave as acids when they are dissolved in water.

- A hydrogen ion is a proton so acids produce **hydrated protons**.

- Acids are **proton donors** (Lowry and Brønsted).

- **Bases** are substances that **neutralise** an acid to produce a salt and water.

- Bases are **proton acceptors** (Lowry and Brønsted).

- **Alkalis** are soluble bases.

- Alkalis dissociate in water to produce OH^- ions (Arrhenius).

- **Strong acids** and **strong bases** are almost 100% ionised in water.

- **Weak acids** and **weak bases** are only slightly ionised in water.

- The **pH scale** is a way of measuring the concentration of hydrogen ions in a solution.

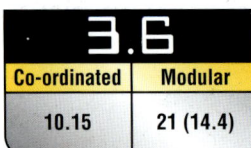

Co-ordinated	Modular
10.15	21 (14.4)

3.6 Making salts

Reacting a base with an acid

When an acid reacts with a base, the products are a **salt** and water. Because acids only behave as acids when they are dissolved in water, water is always present in the reactants in a neutralisation reaction such as this. We can therefore ignore water when we consider the products of the reaction. In effect the method produces just a salt. To ensure that the salt produced is pure, it is vital that there is no excess acid or base dissolved in the solution.

Using an insoluble base

Because the base is not soluble in water, it is easy to ensure that there is no excess acid or base in the final solution of the product salt. If excess base is added, all the acid will be neutralised. The unreacted base can then be removed by filtration leaving just a solution of the salt.

This method does not work if the salt produced is insoluble in water so it could not be used to make lead(II) sulphate.

Making copper(II) sulphate from copper(II) oxide and dilute sulphuric acid

$$H_2SO_4(aq) + CuO(s) \rightarrow CuSO_4(aq) + H_2O(l)$$

Figure 3.25
Copper(II) sulphate is prepared by dissolving copper oxide in dilute sulphuric acid

The stages involved in this process are summarised below:

a) A beaker containing 50 ml of 2M sulphuric acid is heated and copper(II) oxide is slowly added. After each addition, the mixture is stirred until the copper(II) oxide has dissolved. The solution turns blue and each addition of copper(II) oxide increases the intensity of the blue colour as more copper(II) sulphate is formed. It takes about 8 g of copper(II) oxide to neutralise the acid completely.

b) Once that quantity has been added, all the sulphuric acid has been neutralised. The solution is filtered to remove the unreacted copper(II) oxide.

c) The solution is then boiled to remove some of the water. When the total volume is down to about 20 ml, the beaker is left to cool.

d) Blue crystals of copper(II) sulphate are produced as the solution evaporates.

Using a metal carbonate

This method is essentially the same as the method above. The only obvious difference is that carbon dioxide gas is given off in the process. This method also does not work if the salt produced is insoluble in water so it could not be used to make calcium sulphate.

Making copper(II) chloride from copper(II) carbonate and dilute hydrochloric acid

$$2HCl(aq) + CuCO_3(s) \rightarrow CuCl_2(aq) + H_2O(l) + CO_2(g)$$

Figure 3.26
Copper(II) chloride is prepared by dissolving copper(II) carbonate in dilute hydrochloric acid

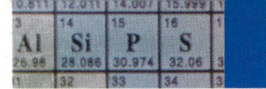

Using a soluble base

With a soluble base it is more difficult to make sure that neither reactant is in excess. If the concentrations of the two solutions are accurately known, the correct volumes can be calculated. The volume of acid and alkali that neutralise each other can be measure by a method called **titration**.

Figure 3.27
A pipette and a burette are used when carrying out a titration

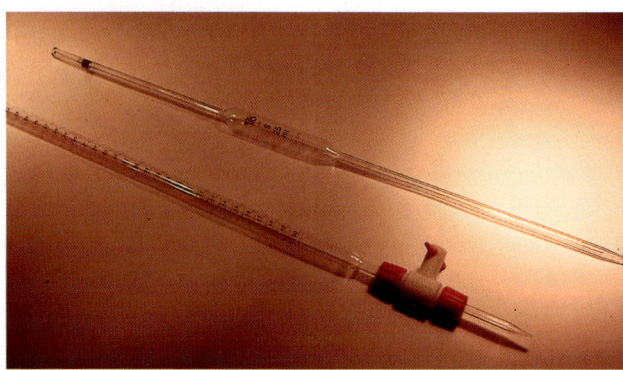

In a titration, a volume of alkali, measured accurately with a **pipette**, is added to a conical flask and a few drops of a suitable **indicator** are added. (Litmus is not an ideal indicator for this process. It is better to use methyl orange or phenolphthalein.) Acid from a **burette** is now added carefully until the indicator changes colour. The volume of acid used is measured. The same volumes of alkali and acid used in the titration are now mixed together – this time without any indicator, which would contaminate the salt.

Making sodium chloride from sodium hydroxide solution and dilute hydrochloric acid

$$NaOH(aq) + HCl(aq) \rightarrow NaCl(aq) + H_2O(l)$$

The stages involved in this process are summarised below:

a) 25 ml of sodium hydroxide are added to a conical flask using a pipette. A few drops of indicator (phenolphthalein) are added.

b) The mixture is titrated with dilute hydrochloric acid from the burette. The acid is added until the indicator changes colour. (With phenolphthalein the change is pink to colourless.)

c) The titration is then repeated but without the indicator. The same volumes of each reactant are used to ensure that neither reactant is in excess.

d) The solution is then poured into an evaporating dish and evaporated to dryness. (It is not possible to crystallise sodium chloride by allowing a solution to cool because the solubility of sodium chloride is not very temperature dependant (see Figure 3.15.)

Reacting a metal with an acid

This process is essentially the same as using an insoluble base. Excess metal is added to neutralise all the acid and the excess removed by filtration.

This method does not work for every metal. Metals lower than hydrogen in the **reactivity series** will not displace hydrogen from acids, so copper and silver salts cannot be made this way.

The reaction is usually:

Figure 3.28
Sodium chloride is prepared by titrating sodium hydroxide with hydrochloric acid

metal + acid → metal salt + hydrogen

Figure 3.29
Iron(II) sulphate is prepared by adding iron filings to sulphuric acid

Making iron(II) sulphate from iron and dilute sulphuric acid

$$H_2SO_4(aq) + Fe(s) \rightarrow FeSO_4(aq) + H_2(g)$$

The stages involved in this process are summarised below:

a) A beaker containing 50 ml of 2M sulphuric acid is heated and iron filings are slowly added. After each addition, the mixture is stirred until the iron has dissolved. Hydrogen gas is produced and the mixture bubbles quite a lot. (Other gases are also given off because there are impurities in the iron. These gases include hydrogen sulphide so the mixture has an unpleasant smell.) The solution turns pale blue-green. It takes about 6 g of iron to neutralise the acid completely.

b) Once that quantity has been added, all the sulphuric acid has been neutralised. The solution is filtered to remove the unreacted iron filings.

c) The solution is then boiled to remove some of the water. When the total volume is down to about 20 ml, the beaker is left to cool.

d) Green-blue crystals of iron(II) sulphate are produced as the solution evaporates.

NOTE

If weak acids are used in this method, the rate of reaction is very slow. This is because the key reaction is:

metal + hydrogen ions → metal ions + hydrogen

In this reaction the hydrogen ions are one of the reactants. In weak acids the hydrogen ion concentration will be very low so the rate of reaction will be slow. You can actually distinguish between strong and weak acids by the rate of their reaction with a suitable metal like magnesium.

Making an insoluble salt by precipitation

Figure 3.30
Marble chips dissolve more rapidly in dilute hydrochloric acid (a) than in dilute sulphuric acid (b)

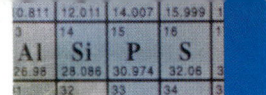

As a general rule, insoluble salts cannot be prepared by reacting an insoluble base or a metal in dilute acid. A good example of this is shown in Figure 3.30. Marble chips (calcium carbonate) dissolve rapidly in hydrochloric acid but very slowly in sulphuric acid of the same concentration. This is because in sulphuric acid, the marble chip gets covered with a layer of insoluble calcium sulphate that reduces the effective surface area of the chip and slows down the reaction.

Insoluble salts like calcium sulphate are best prepared by **precipitation** reactions. In this process separate solutions each containing one of the ions present in the insoluble salt are mixed. The reaction is:

$$\text{metal ion}^+(aq) + \text{'acid' ion}^-(aq) \rightarrow \text{salt}(s)$$

With this method there is no need to worry about using exactly the right amount of each reactant. The insoluble salt produced is filtered out. Any contaminating reactant can easily be removed by washing the insoluble salt with water. This process also removes the other soluble product formed in the reaction.

Making lead(II) iodide by precipitation

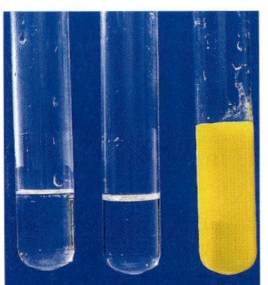

Figure 3.31
Insoluble lead(II) iodide is made by mixing solutions of potassium iodide and lead nitrate

$$Pb(NO_3)_2(aq) + 2KI(aq) \rightarrow 2KNO_3(aq) + PbI_2(s)$$

The stages involved in the process are summarised below:

a) 10 ml of potassium iodide solution are mixed with an equal volume of lead(II) nitrate solution.

b) The resulting mixture is filtered. The potassium nitrate solution (and any excess reactant) is washed out with cold water.

c) Pure lead(II) iodide is left in the filter paper.

Making an anhydrous salt by direct combination of elements

This method can only be used to make salts where the **anion** (negative ion) is a single element. This means that it is particularly useful for making metal halides. Both aluminium and iron(III) chloride can be made this way. (It is not possible to make iron(III) chloride by dissolving iron in hydrochloric acid. The product of this reaction is iron(II) chloride.)

Because this method uses dry reactants, the salt produced is **anhydrous**.

Did you know?

Most salts contain water molecules locked inside the crystal structure. This water is called water of crystallisation. The amount of water of crystallisation is shown in the formula of the salt. For example copper(II) sulphate has 5 molecules of water to every 'molecule' of copper(II) sulphate and its formula is written: $CuSO_4.5H_2O$. In copper(II) sulphate, 36.0% of the crystal's mass is water. Other examples are:

$FeSO_4.7H_2O$ containing 45.3% water by mass.
$CaCl_2.6H_2O$ containing 49.3% water by mass.
$Na_2CO_3.10H_2O$ containing 62.9% water by mass.

Anhydrous salts contain no water of crystallisation. Some, like sodium chloride, only form anhydrous salts, others can exist in both forms. Hydrated copper(II) sulphate exists as blue crystals; anhydrous copper(II) sulphate is a white powder. If water is added to anhydrous copper(II) sulphate it reverts back to the blue, hydrated form. This is the familiar test for water.

0.811	12.011	14.007	15.999	1
3	14	15	16	1
Al	Si	P	S	3
26.98	28.085	30.974	32.06	3
1	32	33	34	3

Making aluminium chloride by directly combining aluminium and chlorine

$$2Al(s) + 3Cl_2(g) \rightarrow 2AlCl_3(s)$$

The stages involved in this process are summarised below:

a) Aluminium turnings (or coarse powder) are placed in a tube. A suitable container is fixed to the end of the tube and chlorine gas is passed over the aluminium. (**CAUTION:** Chlorine is toxic and this method can *only* be done in a fume cupboard.)

b) The aluminium is heated in the stream of chlorine.

c) Anhydrous aluminium chloride is collected in the container.

Figure 3.32
Aluminium chloride is prepared by passing chlorine gas over aluminium turnings

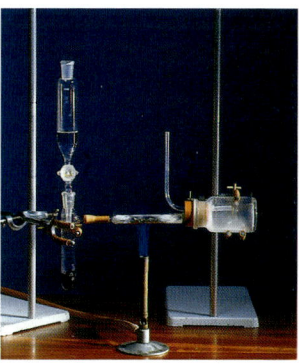

Topic question

1   Outline a method for making reasonably pure samples of the following salts starting with the substance listed. You may also use sulphuric acid, hydrochloric acid or nitric acid. For each method give an equation.

All the salts are soluble in water except silver chloride.

a) Zinc sulphate starting with zinc metal.
b) Potassium chloride starting with a solution of potassium hydroxide.
c) Lead(II) nitrate starting with lead(II) carbonate. (Lead carbonate is not soluble in water.)
d) Magnesium sulphate starting with magnesium oxide. (Magnesium oxide is not soluble in water.)
e) Silver chloride starting with silver nitrate solution.

Summary

◆ Salts can be made by several processes:
   a)   by reacting an acid with a base.
   b)   by reacting an acid with a metal carbonate.
   c)   by reacting an acid with a metal.
   d)   by the direct combination of two elements to produce metal chlorides.

   Not every one of these processes can be used to produce every salt.

◆ Insoluble salts can be produced by precipitation.

3.7	
Co-ordinated	**Modular**
10.15	21 (14.5)

Measuring the concentration of solutions

Doing a titration

The titration method that was used to prepare salts can be used to measure the concentration of a solution. The following method is used.

a) Using an accurate pipette, a volume of one of the reagents is transferred to a clean vessel (usually a conical flask).

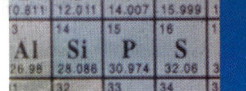

Figure 3.33
Carrying out a titration

b) A few drops of indicator solution are added to the flask. (It is easier to see the endpoint if the colour is not too intense. If the colour seems rather pale it is always possible to add more later.)

c) The other reagent is placed in a burette. The liquid must be run through the burette until the tap and the jet are filled. (The burette does not have to be filled to the 0.0 mark.) The exact initial reading is taken. Figure 3.34 shows how to read a burette.

Always:

    i)   Get the eye level with the meniscus.
    ii)   Read to the bottom of the meniscus.
    ii)   Record the reading.

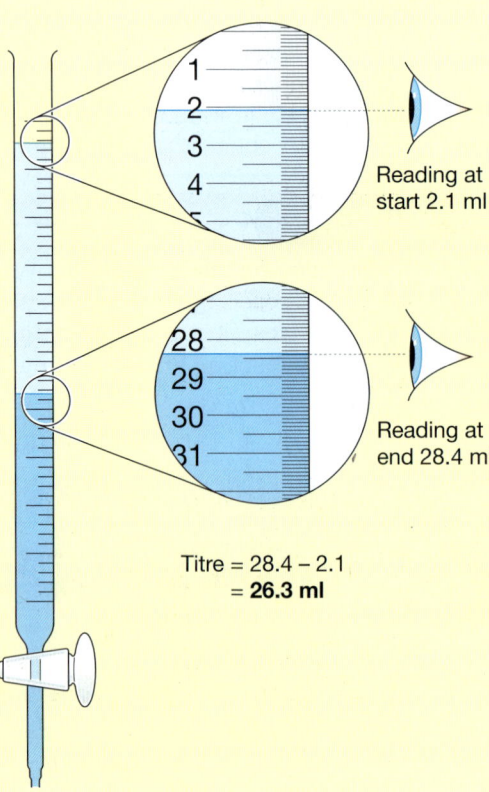

Reading at start 2.1 ml

Reading at end 28.4 ml

Titre = 28.4 − 2.1
= **26.3 ml**

Figure 3.34
The correct way to read a burette

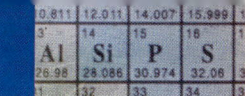

d) The liquid in the burette is added carefully to the contents of the titrating flask. The flask must be swirled to make sure the contents are well mixed.

e) When the endpoint is reached, the burette is read again.

f) The titre is calculated by subtracting the first reading from the second reading.

g) The first titre value will not be very accurate – it is a 'ranging shot' – so the entire process is repeated. This time when the endpoint is near, the liquid from the burette is added drop by drop. (It should be possible to get the titration accurate to the nearest drop (about 0.05 ml).)

h) The titration flask is washed out with distilled water and the titration is repeated. Repeats are made until two or more values for the titre are obtained that are the same to within 0.05 ml.

i) Only these accurate values should be used in the calculation.

Titrations can be used in this way to find the concentrations of one of the reactants if the concentration of the other is known.

Did you know?

The titration method can be used for determining concentration in any reaction where there is a detectable change in the mixture as the reaction is completed. In acid/base titrations the change is detected by the addition of a suitable indicator. Titrations can be used in:

- redox reactions involving transition metals where one of the reagents changes colour.

- reactions where iodine is either liberated or used (the colour change can be enhanced by the use of starch as an indicator).

- reactions between the silver ion $Ag^+(aq)$ and halide ions. Silver halide is precipitated. The end point is determined using a few drops of potassium chromate which goes brick red when all the halide ions have been used and free silver ions are present.

Other methods for detecting the end point include monitoring the electrical conductivity of the solution, measuring the pH of the solution using a meter rather than indicators and measuring the temperature change during a reaction.

The mole

A mole of any substance is the **relative atomic mass** (elements) or the **relative formula mass** (compounds) in grams.

Examples

a) The relative atomic mass of sodium is 23. This can be written as A_r (Na) = 23. So one mole of sodium atoms is 23 grams.

b) The relative atomic mass of oxygen is 16. So A_r (O) = 16. One mole of oxygen atoms is 16 grams.

c) The relative atomic mass of hydrogen is 1. So A_r (H) = 1. Three moles of hydrogen atoms is 3 × 1 grams = 3 grams.

d) For sulphur, A_r (S) = 32. So 0.3 moles of sulphur atoms is 0.3 × 32 grams = 9.6 grams.

e) Oxygen gas exists as O_2 molecules. The relative formula mass of oxygen gas (written as $M_r(O_2)$) is 2 × 16 = 32. One mole of oxygen gas (or oxygen molecules) is 32 grams.

NOTE: One mole of oxygen molecules is *not* the same as one mole of oxygen atoms. It is necessary to state *exactly* what the substance is. To say '1 mole of oxygen' is unclear – does it mean atoms or molecules?

f) One mole of hydrogen gas (or hydrogen molecules H_2) is 2 × 1 = 2. So $M_r(H_2)$ = 2 and one mole of hydrogen gas = 2 grams.

g) The formula of sodium hydroxide is NaOH. One molecule of sodium hydroxide contains:

- 1 sodium atom A_r (Na) = 23
- 1 oxygen atom A_r (O) = 16
- 1 hydrogen atom A_r (H) = 1

So M_r(NaOH) = (1 × 23) + (1 × 16) + (1 × 1) = 40.

One mole of sodium hydroxide has a mass of 40 grams
and 0.6 moles of sodium hydroxide has a mass of 0.6 × 40 = 24 grams.

h) The formula of sulphuric acid is H_2SO_4. One molecule of sulphuric acid contains:

- 2 hydrogen atoms A_r (H) = 1
- 1 sulphur atom A_r (S) = 32
- 4 oxygen atoms A_r (O) = 16

So $M_r(H_2SO_4)$ is (2 × 1) + (1 × 32) + (4 × 16) = 98

One mole of sulphuric acid has a mass of 98 grams and 1.5 moles of sulphuric acid has a mass of 1.5 × 98 = 147 grams

This relationship can also be worked in the opposite direction.

$M_r(Na_2S)$ is (2 × 23) + (1 × 32) = 78.

78 grams of sodium sulphide is 1 mole
so 1 gram of sodium sulphide is $\frac{1}{78}$ moles
and 234 grams of sodium sulphide is $\frac{234}{78}$ = 3 moles

The general rule

$$\text{Number of moles} = \frac{\text{Mass/g}}{A_r \text{ or } M_r}$$

Using the mole in concentrations

The concentration of aqueous solutions is normally expressed in moles per cubic decimetre (mol dm^{-3}). (Notice that the symbol for 'mole' is 'mol'.) This is also called the molarity of the solution and has the symbol M.

So a solution containing 3 moles of solute in 1 cubic decimetre of solution has a concentration of 3 mol dm^{-3}. It is a 3 molar solution (3M solution).

Examples

a) 0.2 mol of H_2SO_4 is present in 1 dm^3 of solution.
The concentration is 0.2 mol dm^{-3} or 0.2M.

b) 500 ml of a solution contains 0.8 mol of NaOH.
So 1000 ml (1 dm^3) of solution would contain:

$$\frac{1000}{500} \times 0.8 = 1.6 \text{ mol of NaOH}$$

The concentration is 1.6 mol dm^{-3} (1.6M).

c) A solution of potassium chloride (KCl) has a concentration of 0.3M. What mass of KCl is present in 10 ml of this solution? [$A_r(K) = 39$, $A_r(Cl) = 35.5$]

$M_r(KCl) = (1 \times 39) + (1 \times 35.5) = 74.5$

So 1 mole is 74.5 grams.

A 0.3M solution contains 0.3 mole in 1 dm^3 of solution

$$0.3 \text{ mole} = 0.3 \times 74.5 \text{ g}$$
$$= 22.35 \text{ g}$$

So 1 dm^3 (1000 ml) of solution contains 22.35 g
and 10 ml contains:

$$22.35 \times \frac{10}{1000}$$

$$= 0.2235 \text{ g}$$

The general rule

v ml of a M molar solution (M mol dm^{-3}) contains

$$\frac{v \times M}{1000} \times M_r \text{ g of solute}$$

Calculating concentrations from titrations

If the concentration of the solution of one of the reactants is known, a titration can be used to determine the concentration of the other reactant.

Examples

a) In a titration, 25 ml of NaOH were neutralised by 26.3 ml of 0.1M HCl. What is the concentration of the NaOH?

i) The equation is:

$$NaOH + HCl \rightarrow NaCl + H_2O$$

ii) The base:

Call the concentration of the NaOH c mol dm^{-3}

25 ml of the solution contain:

$$\frac{25 \times c}{1000} \text{ moles of NaOH}$$

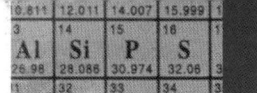
iii) The acid:

26.3 ml of 0.1M HCl contain:

$$\frac{26.3 \times 0.1}{1000} \text{ moles of HCl}$$

iv) Equating the concentrations

From the equation, 1 mole of NaOH is neutralised by 1 mole of HCl.

So:

$$\frac{25 \times c}{1000} = \frac{26.3 \times 0.1}{1000}$$

Cancelling the 1000s gives:

$$25 \times c = 26.3 \times 0.1$$

$$c = \frac{26.3 \times 0.1}{25} = 0.1052 \text{ mol dm}^{-3}$$

The titration is only accurate to $\pm$ 0.05 ml which is a percentage error of $\pm \left(\frac{0.05}{26.3}\right) \times 100 = 0.2\%$ so it is only possible to quote the concentration to this level of accuracy.

The concentration is **0.105 mol dm^{-3}**.

b) In a titration, 20 ml of 0.24M KOH were neutralised by 11.5 ml of H_2SO_4. What is the concentration of the H_2SO_4?

i) The equation is:

$$2KOH + H_2SO_4 \rightarrow K_2SO_4 + 2H_2O$$

ii) The base:

20 ml of the solution contain:

$$\frac{20 \times 0.24}{1000} \text{ moles of KOH}$$

iii) The acid:

Call the concentration of the H_2SO_4 a mol dm^{-3}

11.5 ml of 0.1M H_2SO_4 contain:

$$\frac{11.5 \times a}{1000} \text{ moles of } H_2SO_4$$

iv) Equating the concentrations:

From the equation, 2 moles of KOH are neutralised by 1 mole of H_2SO_4.

So 1 mole of KOH is neutralised by 0.5 mole of H_2SO_4

so:

$$\frac{20 \times 0.24}{1000} \text{ are neutralised by: } 0.5 \times \frac{20 \times 0.24}{1000} \text{ moles of } H_2SO_4$$

Equating the number of moles of H_2SO_4

$$= 0.5 \times \frac{20 \times 0.24}{1000} = \frac{11.5 \times a}{1000}$$

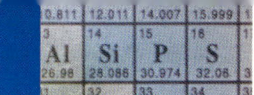

Cancelling the 1000s gives:

$$0.5 \times 20 \times 0.24 = 11.5 \times a$$

$$a = \frac{0.5 \times 20 \times 0.24}{11.5} = 0.209 \text{ mol dm}^{-3}$$

The concentration is **0.209 mol dm^{-3}**.

The general rule

c) In a titration, V_A ml of M_A M acid (M_A mol dm^{-3}) were neutralised by V_B ml of M_B M base (M_B mol dm^{-3}).

   i) The balanced chemical equation is:

$$\textbf{a} \text{ ACID} + \textbf{b} \text{ BASE} \rightarrow \text{products}$$

   a moles of acid are neutralised by **b** moles of base

   ii) The base:

   V_B ml of the solution contain:

$$\frac{V_B \times M_B}{1000} \text{ moles of base}$$

   iii) The acid:

   V_A ml of the solution contain:

$$\frac{V_A \times M_A}{1000} \text{ moles of acid}$$

   iv) Equating the concentrations:

   From the equation, **b** mole of base are neutralised by **a** mole of acid.

   So 1 mole of base is neutralised by $^a/_b$ mole of acid.

   So:

$$\frac{V_B \times M_B}{1000} \text{ of base are neutralised by: } \frac{\textbf{a}}{\textbf{b}} \times \frac{V_B \times M_B}{1000} \text{ moles of acid}$$

   Equating the number of moles of acid:

$$\frac{\textbf{a}}{\textbf{b}} \times \frac{V_B \times M_B}{1000} = \frac{V_A \times M_A}{1000}$$

   Cancelling the 1000s gives:

$$\frac{\textbf{a}}{\textbf{b}} \times V_B \times M_B = V_A \times M_A$$

   which can be rearranged to:

$$\frac{V_B \times M_B}{\textbf{b}} = \frac{V_A \times M_A}{\textbf{a}}$$

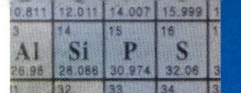

Topic questions

1   In a titration the following results are obtained:

burette reading	1st titration	2nd titration	3rd titration	4th titration
2nd reading	21.85	21.95	22	21.85
1st reading	0.15	0.4	0.55	0.3
titre				

Calculate the titre values and decide the correct value to use in a calculation.

In the following calculations use these values for the relative atomic masses.

H = 1; C = 12; N = 14; O = 16; Na = 23; S = 32; Cl = 35.5; K = 39; Ca = 40

2   What is the mass of:
a) 1 mol of sulphur atoms?
b) 2 mol of chlorine molecules?
c) 0.5 mol of water molecules?
d) 1.35 mol of hydrochloric acid molecules?

3   How many moles are in:
a) 46 g of sodium atoms?
b) 3.9 g of potassium atoms?
c) 1.98 g of water molecules?
d) 0.803 g of hydrogen chloride molecules?

4   What is the molar concentration of the following solutions?
a) 2 g of sodium hydroxide in 1 litre of solution.
b) 3.15 g of nitric acid in 500 ml of solution.
c) 0.49 g of sulphuric acid in 2 litres of solution.

5   How many grams of solute are present in the following solutions?
a) 100 ml of 2M sodium chloride solution.
b) 0.25 ml of 1M potassium carbonate solution.
c) 1.5 litres of 0.01M sulphuric acid.
d) 52.5 ml of 0.15M ammonia solution. (Ammonia is NH_3).

6   Calculate the missing values in the following:
a) 20 ml of 0.1M HCl(aq) neutralise 22.1 ml of _____ M NaOH(aq).

b) 25 ml of 0.05M H_2SO_4(aq) neutralise _____ ml of 0.15M KOH(aq).

c) _____ ml of 0.12M HNO_3(aq) neutralise 15 ml of 0.1M $Ca(OH)_2$(aq)

Summary

- A mole of any substance is the relative atomic mass (or relative formula mass) of that substance in grams.

- The number of moles of a substance
$$= \frac{\text{mass of substance (in grams)}}{\text{relative atomic (or formula) mass}}$$

- The molarity of a solution is the number of moles of solute in 1 dm^3 (litre) of solution.

- The number of moles of solute in v ml of a M molar solution $= \dfrac{v \times M}{1000}$

- The number of grams of solute in v ml of a M molar solution
$$= \frac{v \times M}{1000} \times M_r \text{ g of solute}$$

- In a neutralisation reaction if a moles of acid A exactly neutralise b moles of base B and V_A ml of a M_A molar solution of acid A exactly neutralise V_B ml of a M_B molar solution of base B then:
$$\frac{(V_A \times M_A)}{a} = \frac{(V_B \times M_B)}{b}$$

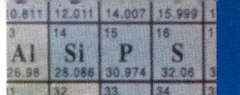

Examination questions

1 This question is about the water cycle.
The water cycle can be described in nine sentences.
In the cycle below, five of the sentences are missing.
These five missing sentences are given in the list below in the **wrong** order.

A These rise further and cool.
B This heat evaporates the water producing water vapour.
C As this happens, clouds are formed.
D This water vapour rises into the atmosphere.
E This cooling causes water droplets to form rain.

Complete the description of the water cycle by writing the letters **A**, **B**, **C**, **D** and **E** in the boxes in the correct order.

'The Water Cycle'

- The water cycle starts with water in rivers, lakes and oceans.
- This water is warmed by the heat of the sun.
- ☐
- ☐
- ☐
- ☐
- ☐
- This falls from the sky onto seas and land.
- The water cycle begins again. *(3 marks)*

2 The label shows the ions present in the bottle of spring water. This water is *temporarily* hard.

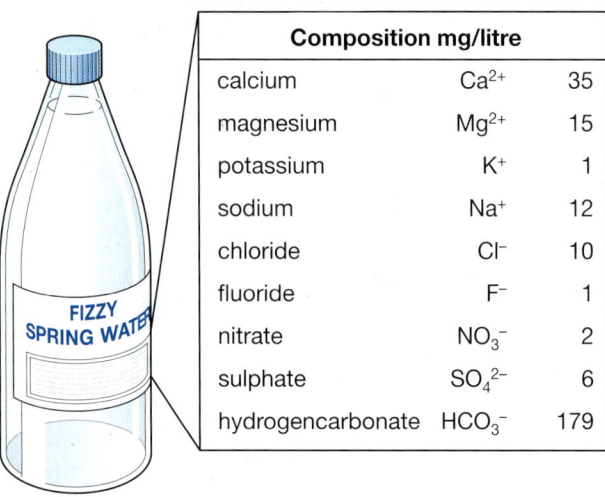

Composition mg/litre		
calcium	Ca^{2+}	35
magnesium	Mg^{2+}	15
potassium	K^+	1
sodium	Na^+	12
chloride	Cl^-	10
fluoride	F^-	1
nitrate	NO_3^-	2
sulphate	SO_4^{2-}	6
hydrogencarbonate	HCO_3^-	179

a) Name the compound that would be present in the greatest amount if this water were evaporated to dryness. *(2 marks)*

b) i) What is hard water? *(2 marks)*
   ii) State one advantage of hard water. *(1 mark)*

c) Describe an experiment that would show that this water is *temporarily* hard. *(4 marks)*

d) This hard water may be softened as shown.

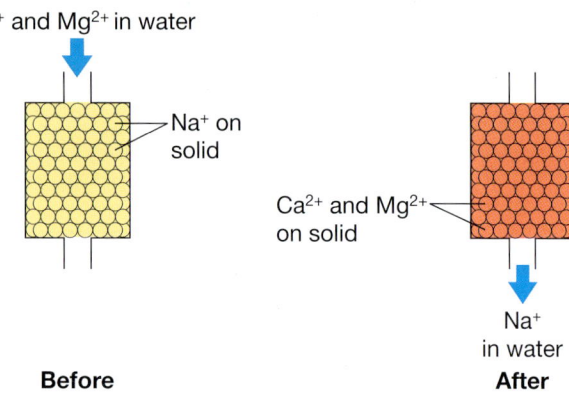

Before　　　　**After**

What name is given to this process? *(1 mark)*

3 a) Explain what is meant by
   i) a **saturated** solution *(2 marks)*
   ii) a **saturated** hydrocarbon *(1 mark)*

b) The table shows some data for the solubility of ammonium chloride in water at different temperatures.

Temperature (°C)	Solubility (g per 100 g water)
0	29.4
20	37.2
40	40.5
60	55.2
80	65.6
100	77.3

Select a suitable scale for each axis and plot the data on a grid like the one shown.
Draw a smooth curve to show how the solubility of ammonium chloride in water changes with temperature, allowing for any anomalous point.

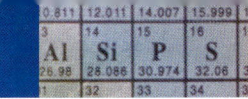

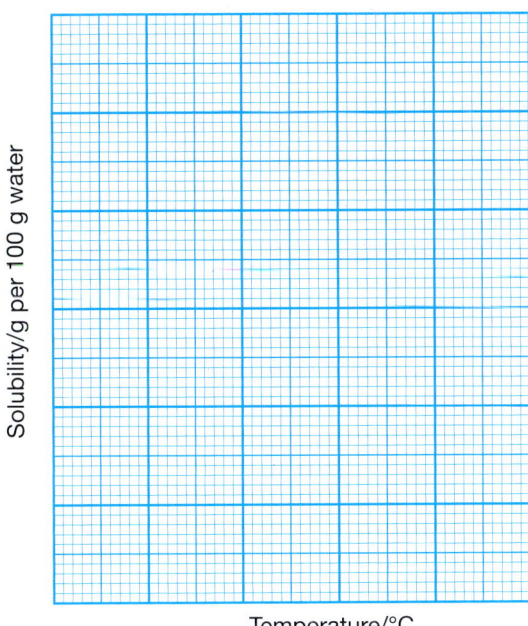

Solubility/g per 100 g water

Temperature/°C

(3 marks)

c) Use your graph to answer the following questions.

   i)   What is the solubility of ammonium chloride at 90°C? *(1 mark)*

   ii) What is the lowest temperature at which 50 g of ammonium chloride dissolves completely in 100 g of water? *(1 mark)*

   iii) What mass of ammonium chloride crystals would be obtained if a saturated solution of ammonium chloride, prepared using 50 g of water, was cooled from 100°C to 30°C? *(2 marks)*

4 Ethanoic acid, CH_3COOH, forms a *weak acid* when added to water. Some reactions of ethanoic acid are shown.

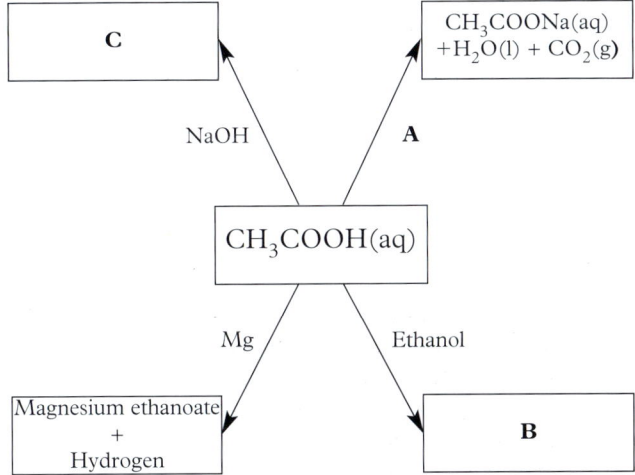

a) Explain what is meant by a *weak acid*. *(2 marks)*

b) Name the substance **A** that is added to ethanoic acid. *(1 mark)*

c) Substance **B** is formed when ethanoic acid reacts with ethanol. What type of substance is **B**? *(1 mark)*

d) Draw a displayed structural formula for salt **C**. *(1 mark)*

e) Write a balanced chemical equation for the reaction between magnesium and ethanoic acid. *(2 marks)*

5 Salts can be made by neutralising acids. A student followed these instructions to make common salt, sodium chloride.

a)

Instruction 1 – Put 10 cm³ of hydrochloric acid in a beaker. Test one drop of the solution with Universal Indicator paper.

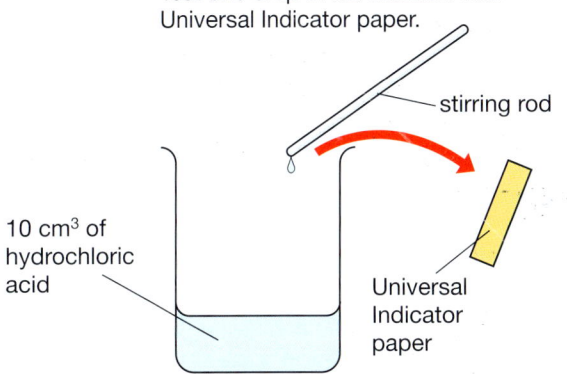

What colour would the Universal Indicator paper go? *(1 mark)*

b)

Instruction 2 – Add 9 cm³ of sodium hydroxide solution to the beaker. Stir and test one drop of the solution with Universal Indicator paper.

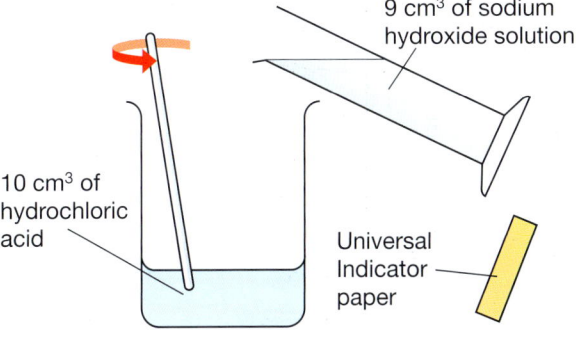

The colour of the Universal Indicator paper was the same as in (a). Why? *(1 mark)*

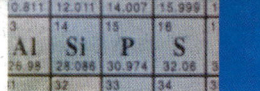

c)

Instruction 3 – Now add more sodium hydroxide solution a drop at a time. Stir the solution each time and test with Universal Indicator paper.

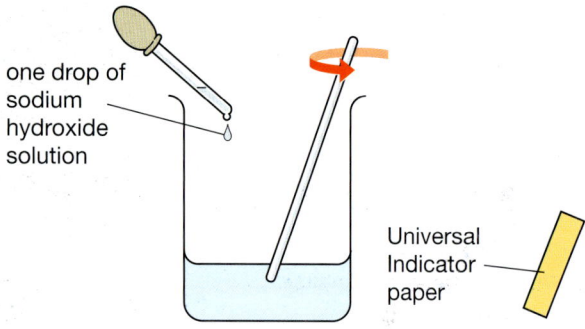

one drop of sodium hydroxide solution

Universal Indicator paper

i) The Universal Indicator paper showed that the solution was now alkaline. What should be done to make the solution neutral? *(1 mark)*

ii) When the solution was neutral, what colour and pH was shown by the Universal Indicator paper? *(2 marks)*

d) The equation for the reaction is:

$$NaOH(aq) + HCl(aq) \rightarrow NaCl(aq) + H_2O(l)$$

i) What is the chemical formula of hydrochloric acid? *(1 mark)*

ii) Sodium chloride crystals often form in the neutral solution. Explain how. *(2 marks)*

iii) Sodium chloride for use in the home is not prepared by this reaction. Explain why. *(2 marks)*

6 An oven cleaner solution contained sodium hydroxide. A 25.0 cm³ sample of the oven cleaner solution was placed in a flask. The sample was titrated with hydrochloric acid containing 73 g/dm³ of hydrogen chloride, HCl.
a) Describe how this titration is carried out. *(3 marks)*

b) Calculate the concentration of the hydrochloric acid in mol/dm³.
Relative atomic masses: H 1; Cl 35.5 *(2 marks)*

c) 10.0 cm³ of hydrochloric acid were required to neutralise the 25.0 cm³ of oven cleaner solution.
  i)   Calculate the number of moles of hydrochloric acid reacting. *(2 marks)*
  ii) Calculate the concentration of sodium hydroxide in the oven cleaner solution in mol/dm³. *(2 marks)*

7 A student carried out a titration to find the concentration of a solution of sulphuric acid. 25.0 cm³ of the sulphuric acid solution was neutralised exactly by 34.0 cm³ of a potassium hydroxide solution of concentration 2.0 mol/dm³. The equation for the reaction is

$$2KOH(aq) + H_2SO_4(aq) \rightarrow K_2SO_4(aq) + 2H_2O(l)$$

a) Describe the experimental procedure for the titration carried out by the student. *(4 marks)*

b) Calculate the number of moles of potassium hydroxide used. *(2 marks)*

c) Calculate the concentration of the sulphuric acid in mol/dm³. *(3 marks)*

Chapter 4

Detection and identification

Key terms

flame test • gas chromatography • ion •
mass spectrometry • molar • nuclear magnetic resonance •
precipitate • spectroscopy •
thermal decomposition

4.1	
Co-ordinated	**Modular**
10.16	22 (15.4)

Laboratory methods

It is possible to identify almost any substance by chemical methods. The tests mentioned in this section are a sample of the methods that can be used.

Identifying positive ions

Flame tests

In a **flame test** the substance to be tested is placed in a watch glass. A clean platinum wire is placed in the substance and the wire is then touched to the edge of a blue Bunsen flame. Some metal **ions** will colour the flame. Figure 4.1 shows the colours obtained by different elements. These are summarised in Figure 4.2.

Figure 4.1
Certain elements produce certain coloured flames. The elements shown here are a) lithium, b) sodium, c) potassium, d) calcium and e) barium

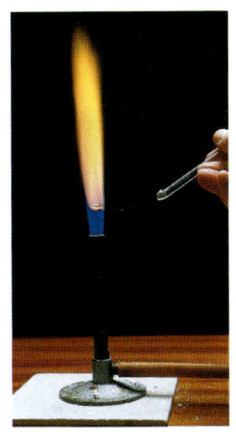

Figure 4.2
The flame colours produced by the five elements from Figure 4.1

Metal ion	Flame colour
lithium (Li^+)	bright red
sodium (Na^+)	golden yellow
potassium (K^+)	lilac
calcium (Ca^{2+})	brick red
barium (Ba^{2+})	apple green

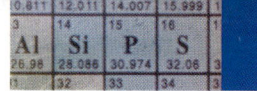

Detection and identification

Other metals like copper and lead also colour the flame. Do not confuse the flame colour in this test with the colour of the flame when the element is burned in oxygen. In some cases the colour is the same (e.g. sodium and calcium), in others it is not. Magnesium metal burns with an intense white flame in oxygen but magnesium compounds do not colour a flame.

Did you know?

When a metal ion is heated, some of the electrons gain enough energy to move into a different electron level. On cooling slightly, the electron drops back to its original level. The energy given out in the drop is often given out as light energy. For some metals the energy given out is in the infrared or ultraviolet parts of the electromagnetic spectrum so the flame has no visible colour.

Adding sodium hydroxide solution

Two or 3 ml of a solution of the substance being tested are placed in a test tube. **Molar** sodium hydroxide is added slowly until it is in excess. Figure 4.3 shows the effect of sodium hydroxide solution on different ions.

Figure 4.3
The effect of sodium hydroxide solution on different ions

Ion present	Effect of adding sodium hydroxide solution	
	A few drops of the solution	An excess of the solution
aluminium (Al^{3+})	white, gelatinous precipitate	precipitate re-dissolves
calcium (Ca^{2+})	white precipitate	no change to precipitate
magnesium (Mg^{2+})	white precipitate	no change to precipitate
copper(II) (Cu^{2+})	blue-green, gelatinous precipitate	no change to precipitate
iron(II) (Fe^{2+})	green-grey, gelatinous precipitate	no change to precipitate
iron(III) (Fe^{3+})	red-brown gelatinous precipitate	no change to precipitate
ammonium (NH_4^+)	ammonia gas given off when heated	

Test for ammonia
Ammonia has a distinctive, pungent odour. The gas turns damp red litmus paper blue

Figure 4.4
The precipitates of the following hydroxides:
a) aluminium hydroxide,
b) magnesium hydroxide,
c) copper(II) hydroxide,
d) iron(III) hydroxide

In each of the reactions with metal ions, the **precipitate** is the metal hydroxide. For the 2+ ions, the reaction is:

$$M^{2+}(aq) + 2NaOH(aq) \rightarrow 2Na^+(aq) + M(OH)_2(s)$$

For the 3+ ions, the reaction is:

$$M^{3+}(aq) + 3NaOH(aq) \rightarrow 3Na^+(aq) + M(OH)_3(s)$$

Aluminium hydroxide re-dissolves in sodium hydroxide to form sodium aluminate solution.

With the ammonium ion, the reaction is:

$$NH_4^+(aq) + NaOH(aq) \rightarrow NH_3(g) + H_2O(l) + Na^+(aq)$$

Identifying negative ions

The standard tests for the common negative ions are shown in Figure 4.5.

Figure 4.5
The standard tests for the common negative ions

Negative ion present	Test	Positive result
carbonate (CO_3^{2-})	add dilute acid	carbon dioxide gas given off
chloride (Cl^-)	add dilute nitric acid *then* add silver nitrate solution	white precipitate
bromide (Br^-)	add dilute nitric acid *then* add silver nitrate solution	cream coloured precipitate
iodide (I^-)	add dilute nitric acid *then* add silver nitrate solution	yellow coloured precipitate
sulphate (SO_4^{2-})	add dilute hydrochloric acid *then* add barium chloride solution	white precipitate
nitrate (NO_3^-) (see note below)	add sodium hydroxide solution *then* add aluminium powder *and* heat the mixture	ammonia gas given off

Note: The nitrate test can't be used if the ammonium ion is present. It is necessary to remove the ammonium ion before testing for the nitrate ion. This can be done by heating the substance with sodium hydroxide until all the ammonia has been evolved *then* adding aluminium powder and heating.

The reactions involved are:

carbonate $$CO_3^{2-}(aq) + 2H^+(aq) \rightarrow H_2O(l) + CO_2(g)$$

chloride $$Cl^-(aq) + Ag^+(aq) \rightarrow AgCl(s)$$

bromide $$Br^-(aq) + Ag^+(aq) \rightarrow AgBr(s)$$

iodide $$I^-(aq) + Ag^+(aq) \rightarrow AgI(s)$$

sulphate $$SO_4^{2-}(aq) + Ba^{2+}(aq) \rightarrow BaSO_4(s)$$

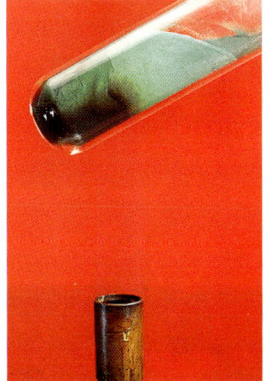

Figure 4.6
When copper(II) carbonate is heated, copper oxide and carbon dioxide are formed

Heating substances

Many substances change when heated. These changes can be used to help in identification. Copper(II) carbonate (which is a green powder) is **thermally decomposed** when heated to produce a black powder and carbon dioxide gas.

$$CuCO_3(s) \rightarrow CuO(s) + CO_2(g)$$

Zinc carbonate (a white powder) also decomposes when heated to produce white zinc oxide and carbon dioxide gas. The zinc oxide produced is yellow when hot but turns white again when it cools.

$$ZnCO_3(s) \rightarrow ZnO(s) + CO_2(g)$$

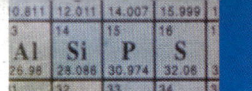

Detection and identification

Figure 4.7
Zinc oxide is yellow when hot and white when cold

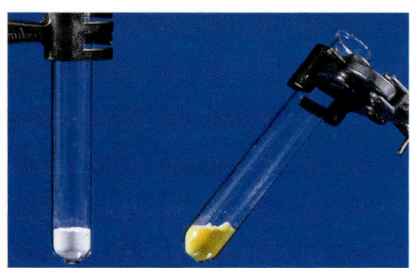

Summary

◆ **Flame tests** can be used to identify many positive ions.

◆ Many positive ions can also be identified by their reaction with sodium hydroxide solution.

◆ Various tests can be used to identify negative ions.

4.2	
Co-ordinated	**Modular**
10.16	22 (15.5)

Instrumental methods

Laboratory methods of identification are slow and need relatively large amounts of material. In contrast, instrumental methods are very quick, accurate and sensitive, and often need only very small amounts of material. The instruments used are, however, very expensive and are only suitable when a lot of testing has to be done.

Using modern electronics and computer technology, instrumental methods have become very efficient. This makes them ideal for industrial use. Steel samples from the furnace can be analysed in minutes. The method used is **spectroscopy**.

Using this method, the accurate analysis is known before the steel is poured from the furnace (see Chapter 2). In the past, using laboratory analysis, the steel had to be solidified then samples taken and analysed. The process could take several days and required very skilled analytical chemists to carry out the work. If the composition was wrong, the steel would have to be re-melted and its composition changed. Re-melting the steel used a lot of energy and was very expensive.

Modern instrumental methods can also keep a rapid and accurate check on the environment. Oil tankers sometimes discharge oil residues from their tanks into the sea causing pollution. Using a combination of **gas chromatography** and **mass spectrometry** it is possible to analyse the contents of oil slicks with such accuracy that the tanker that caused the slick can be positively identified.

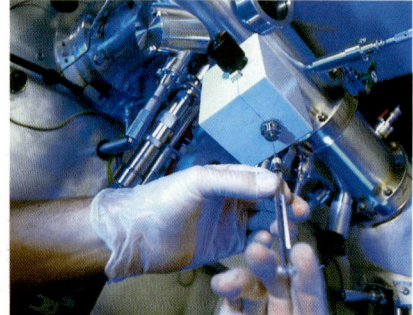

Figure 4.8
A gas chromatograph in use (left)

Figure 4.9
Using a mass spectrometer

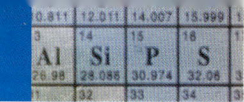

All instrumental methods work by measuring a specific property of an element or compound. Figure 4.10 lists a number of instrumental methods and the scientific principle behind them.

Figure 4.10
Some modern instrumental methods of analysis

Method	Used to identify:	Scientific principle used
nuclear magnetic resonance (NMR)	organic compounds	The hydrogen atoms in organic compounds behave like small magnets. In a magnetic field they absorb electromagnetic energy. The frequency of the energy absorbed depends on what the hydrogen atom is connected to. The presence of functional groups like $-CH_3$, $=CH_2$, $-OH$ etc. can be identified.
mass spectrometry	elements (and their isotopes)	In an electric field, positive ions will move towards the negative electrode. The amount of movement depends on the mass of the ion. (Lighter ions move more.) Measuring the deflection of an ion allows its mass to be determined.
emission spectroscopy	elements	When elements are heated, electrons can get enough energy to move to a higher energy level. When the electrons go back to the lower level they give out this energy as light (or infrared or ultraviolet energy) of a particular frequency. Different elements give out different frequencies. By identifying the frequencies, the elements present can be determined. This is what colours the flames in a flame test.
absorption spectroscopy	elements	This uses the same principle as emission spectroscopy. In this case energy is absorbed to move an electron to a higher level. The spectrum has dark bands at the frequencies absorbed.
infrared spectroscopy	compounds (mainly organic)	This method uses absorption spectroscopy in the infrared region. In this method, energy is absorbed by bonds in the molecules and not electrons in the atoms. Different types of bond absorb energy at different frequencies. So C–H, C = C, C–O and C = O bonds can be identified.
gas chromatography	volatile substances	The method is similar to paper chromatography. In gas chromatography the substance is passed along a tube (instead of a piece of paper) in a carrier gas (instead of a solvent like water or ethanol). The length of time it takes to get to the end of the tube is used to identify the substance.

These methods have been developed over many years. Spectroscopy was first developed by two German scientists (one was Robert Wilhelm von Bunsen – best known for his invention of the laboratory burner) in the 1850s. Mass spectrometry was developed in the 1920s and **nuclear magnetic resonance** (NMR) in the 1950s.

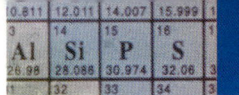

Detection and identification

Figure 4.11
A modern NMR machine

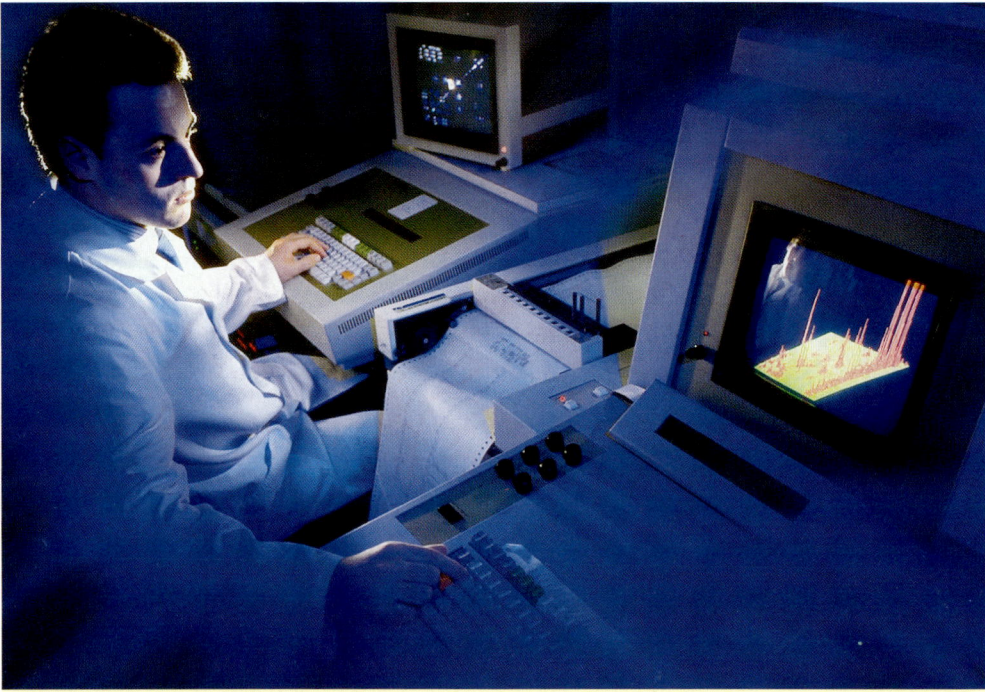

The development of these methods to the sophisticated instruments used today is a result of the fact that the methods have been so useful. They have increased the speed and accuracy of analytical methods. They have resulted in many benefits to society: increased efficiency in industry, more accurate forensic analysis in the fight against crime, better diagnostic methods in medicine etc.

Topic questions

1 In a flame test, what element would be present if the flame had the following colours?
   a) Apple green.
   b) Golden yellow.
   c) Brick red.

2 Sodium hydroxide solution is added to a solution of a metal ion. Which metal ion is present if:
   a) a red-brown precipitate forms?
   b) a blue-green precipitate forms?
   c) a white precipitate forms which re-dissolves when excess sodium hydroxide is added?

3 Give full details of the test you would use for the ammonium ion.

4 Give full details of the test you would use for the carbonate ion.

5 Describe the test for the nitrate ion. What precautions must you take to ensure you don't get a false result?

6 Describe the test for the halide ions. How could you tell which halide was present?

7 Which instrumental method(s) would you use to do the following?

   a) Detect the carboxylic acid functional group (COOH) in a compound.

   b) Analyse a sample of petrol to find out which alkanes were in it.

   c) Prove that chlorine gas contains 75% ^{35}Cl and 25% ^{37}Cl.

Summary

◆ **Instrumental methods**, including spectroscopy, infrared spectroscopy, gas chromatography, mass spectrometry and nuclear magnetic resonance, can be used to identify elements and compounds.

Examination questions

1 A student performed some chemical reactions on **two** compounds.

a) Reactions starting with compound **S**.

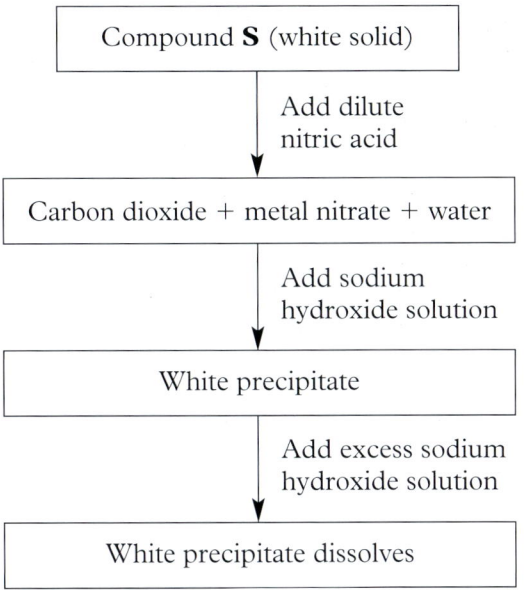

i) What type of chemical reaction occurs when nitric acid reacts with compound **S**? *(1 mark)*

ii) What does the reaction in (i) tell you about compound **S**? *(1 mark)*

iii) Which metal ion is present in compound **S**? Give a reason for your answer. *(2 marks)*

b) Reactions starting with iron(II) sulphate.

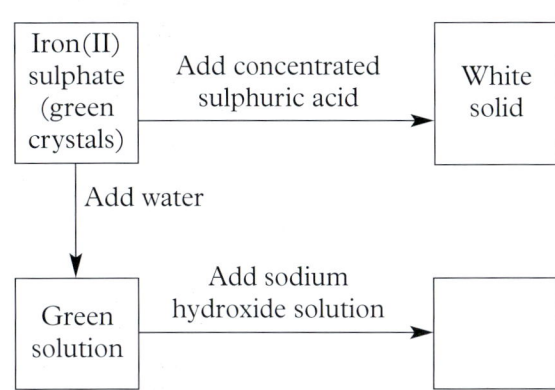

i) Copy the chart and write in the empty box the expected observation when sodium hydroxide solution is added to the green solution. *(1 mark)*

ii) Write a balanced ionic equation for the reaction in (i). *(2 marks)*

iii) What type of chemical reaction occurs when concentrated sulphuric acid is added to crystals or iron(II) sulphate? *(1 mark)*

2 Four bottles are known to contain the following substances of the same concentration.

sodium chloride solution (NaCl)
sodium hydroxide solution (NaOH)
sodium sulphate solution (Na_2SO_4)
ammonia solution (NH_3)

Unfortunately, the labels have come off the bottles.

Describe what **chemical** tests you would do to identify which bottle contained which substance.

Credit will be given for not only describing the tests and stating what you would expect to see, but also for the way you organise your answer.

(4 marks)

Glossary

Acid A substance that dissolves in water to give a solution with a pH of less than 7.

An acid forms hydrogen ions $H^+(aq)$, when added to water and can give up a proton to a base.

Addition polymerisation A reaction in which unsaturated alkene molecules join to form saturated polymer molecules.

Addition reactions Reactions in which monomer molecules link together to produce a polymer and nothing else.

Alcohol A member of a group of compounds containing an –OH group. Often used to mean ethanol, which is the alcohol found in alcoholic drinks.

Alkali A base (metal oxide or hydroxide) that dissolves in water to form a solution with a pH greater than 7.

It is a substance that forms hydroxide ions, $OH^-(aq)$, when added to water.

Alkanes A family of hydrocarbons with the general formula C_nH_{2n+n}. Methane (CH_4) is the simplest alkane. Alkanes have a single covalent bond between the atoms.

Alkenes A family of unsaturated hydrocarbons with the general formula C_nH_{2n}. Ethene (C_2H_4) is the simplest alkene. Alkenes have a double covalent bond between two carbon atoms. Alkenes decolourise bromine water.

Alloy A mixture of metals (or of carbon with a metal). Alloys can have properties different from the parent metal(s).

Anaerobic A process which takes place in the absence of oxygen.

Anhydrous Crystals from which water has been removed.

Anions Atom or groups of atoms that have gained electrons to become negatively-charged ions.

Anode The positively-charged electrode.

Anodising The process of making the protective oxide layer on the surface of aluminium thicker by making the object the anode in a bath of sulphuric acid.

Artificial fertilisers Fertilisers like ammonium nitrate that are not naturally occurring.

Base An oxide or hydroxide of a metal.

Biological catalyst A catalyst found in organisms – usually some type of enzyme.

Blast furnace The industrial method used for extracting metals, such as iron, from their ores.

Boiling point The temperature at which a liquid turns to a gas.

Bond energy The energy (in kJ/mol) needed to break a bond.

Branched chain The arrangement of carbon atoms in organic molecules in which the carbon atoms are not all in a straight chain.

Burette A narrow glass tube with a valve at the bottom to allow the dispensing of accurately measured volumes of liquid.

Carboxylic acids Organic acids containing the –COOH functional group.

Cast iron Iron straight from the blast furnace. Cast iron contains impurities including about 4% carbon.

Catalyst A substance that changes the speed of a reaction but remains unchanged after the reaction.

Cathode The negatively-charged electrode.

Cations Atoms or groups of atoms that have lost electrons to become positively-charged ions.

Complete combustion The burning process of organic fuels in which no carbon monoxide is produced. (The fuel is oxidised as much as possible.)

Contact process The industrial process which converts a mixture of sulphur dioxide and oxygen to sulphur trioxide. The process is used in the manufacture of sulphuric acid.

Corrosion resistant A term used to refer to steels that have a high chromium content (about 15–20%) and which do not rust easily. (Used to be called 'stainless steel'.)

Covalent bond The bonding of atoms caused by the sharing of pairs of electrons in their outer electron shells.

Covalent compounds Compounds in which the atoms are held together by covalent bonds.

Cross-linking bonds Bonds between neighbouring long chain molecules in polymers.

Dehydrating agent Substances (like concentrated sulphuric acid) which can remove water from other substances.

Density A means of comparing the 'heaviness' of different substances. Usually quoted as the mass of a certain volume of the substance (g/ml or kg/m^3).

Double bonds Where two atoms are held together by two bonds instead of just one (e.g. $C = C$, $C = O$).

Electrolysis The process of splitting up a chemical compound using an electric current.

Electrolyte The solution in which electrolysis takes place.

Electrons Negatively-charged sub-atomic particles orbiting in shells around the atomic nucleus.

Electroplating The process of covering materials (usually metals) with a thin layer of another metal.

Enzyme A protein that can act as a catalyst for a reaction. It can be easily destroyed (denatured) by heating.

Esters Organic compounds formed by the reaction between a carboxylic acid and an alcohol. They usually have strong odours and tastes and are present as the flavouring in many foods.

Exothermic Of a reaction in which heat energy is transferred to the surroundings because more energy is given out making the new chemical bonds in the products than is taken in to break the existing bonds in the reactants.

Fermentation The changing of glucose into ethanol (alcohol) and carbon dioxide by the action of enzymes in yeast.

Flame test A way of identifying the metal present in some compounds by means of the colour of a flame.

Functional group Groups in organic molecules that have particular behaviours (e.g. –OH, –COOH).

Gas chromatography A form of chromatography in which gases are identified by the speed they travel along a long tube.

General equation An equation in which a general formula is used not a specific one.

General formula A formula that represents a group of compounds (homologous series) (e.g. the general formula of alkanes which is C_nH_{2n+2}).

Haemoglobin The red pigment in the red blood cells which combines with and transports oxygen.

Hard water Water that contains calcium (Ca^{2+}) or magnesium (Mg^{2+}) ions. Hard water forms a 'scum' with soap.

Homologous series A group of organic compounds that have similar chemical properties (e.g. alcohols, carboxylic acids etc.).

Hydrated proton The name given to the hydrogen ion (H^+) when in water. It can be represented by the symbol $H^+(aq)$. (In some books it is represented by the formula H^+_3O.)

Hydrogenated A compound in which the $C = C$ double bond has been reacted with hydrogen to form a C–C single bond.

Incomplete combustion The burning of organic compounds in an inadequate supply of oxygen so that carbon monoxide gas or elemental carbon are produced instead of carbon dioxide.

Indicator A dye which changes colour when mixed with acidic, alkaline or neutral solutions.

Ion An atom or group of atoms which have lost or gained electrons to become positively or negatively charged.

Ion exchange A process in which one type of ion is removed and replaced by another.

Ionic bond The electrostatic attraction between opposite charges responsible for holding metal and non-metal elements together in a compound. The ions are formed when the metal atoms transfer electrons to the non-metal atoms in order to achieve full outer electron shells.

Ionic compounds Compounds formed by the attraction between ions of opposite charge.

Isomers Organic substances with different structures but the same molecular formula.

Limescale The substance formed on the inside of vessels in which hard water has been heated.

Mass spectrometry A method of identifying elements by measuring the mass of the atoms present.

Melting point The temperature at which a solid turns into a liquid.

Mild steel Steel that contains very little carbon (usually $< 0.3\%$).

Molar The word used to indicate the concentration of a solution (e.g. a solution with a concentration of 2 moles/dm^3 would be called a '2 Molar' (or 2M) solution).

Mole The mass in grams of 6×10^{23} particles of any substance. It is the relative atomic mass of an element or the relative formula mass of a substance expressed in grams.

Molecular formula The basic formula of a compound (usually an organic compound) (e.g. C_2H_6 for ethane) that just indicates what elements are present and their quantity.

Monomers Small molecules which join together to form a long chain of molecules called a polymer.

Neutralisation A reaction between an acid and a base or a carbonate.

Neutralising See neutralisation.

Non-metal Element in the Periodic Table which usually has a low melting point and boiling point, is a poor conductor of electricity and heat, and is brittle as a solid.

Nuclear magnetic resonance A means of identifying the functional groups present in an organic molecule by the way the molecule absorbs energy when in a magnetic field.

Nucleus (atom) The central part of an atom that contains positively-charged protons and uncharged neutrons.

Organic Compounds of carbon found in large quantities in living and dead organisms.

Oxidation A chemical reaction which involves the addition of oxygen.

A reaction involving the loss of electrons.

Oxidise See oxidation.

Permanent hardness Hardness in water that cannot be removed by boiling the water. Usually caused by substances like calcium sulphate.

pH scale A scale used to measure acidity and alkalinity.

Pipette A calibrated tube that can deliver a very precise volume of liquid.

Plastics The common name for polymers.

Polymer A long chain molecule made up of many smaller molecules called monomers.

Precipitate The formation of an insoluble solid during the reaction between two solutions.

Precipitation (chemical) The type of reaction in which a precipitate is formed.

Proton A positively-charged particle found in the nucleus of an atom. It has a mass similar to that of a neutron and the number of protons present decides which element is present.

Proton acceptors Substances which can react with hydrogen ions. (Usually bases.)

Proton donors Substances which contain hydrogen ions. (Usually acids.)

Reactivity series A list of metals arranged in order of their chemical reactivity. The most reactive metals are at the top of the list.

Redox reaction Reactions in which one reactant is REDuced and another is OXidised.

Relative atomic mass The average mass of an atom of an element on a scale on which the mass of a hydrogen atom = 1 or the mass of the ^{12}C isotope of carbon = 12. It takes into account the relative abundance of different isotopes with different mass numbers.

Relative formula mass See relative molecular mass.

Relative molecular mass This is found by adding together the relative atomic masses of all the atoms in one molecule of the substance.

Respiration The process taking place in living cells transferring energy from food molecules (glucose) to cellular energy.

Reversible reaction A reaction that can proceed in either direction depending on the reaction conditions. Reactants can be changed into products which in turn can be changed back into reactants.

Rutile The name of a naturally-occurring ore of the metal titanium (mainly TiO_2).

Salt The name of any substance that contains a positive ion other than H^+ and a negative ion from an acid (e.g. 'common' salt, sodium chloride Na^+Cl^-).

Saturated hydrocarbons Hydrocarbons in which the carbon atoms are all linked together with single C–C bonds.

Saturated solution A solution that contains the maximum amount of solute that will dissolve at that temperature.

Scum The unpleasant 'greasy' material that forms when soap reacts with the calcium and magnesium ions in hard water.

Slag The substance that forms in the blast furnace that contains most of the impurities.

Smelting The process of getting a metal from its ore by heating the ore with carbon.

Soap The salt of a long chain organic acid that is able to disperse oily materials in water.

Soft water Water with no (or very few) calcium and magnesium ions in it.

Solubility A measure of the amount of solute needed to produce a saturated solution. Usually measured as the mass (g) of solute that will dissolve in 100 g of solvent.

Soluble Able to be dissolved (usually in water).

Solute The substance (often a solid) that dissolves in a solvent (usually a liquid) to produce a solution.

Solvent The substance (usually a liquid) into which a solute will dissolve to produce a solution.

Spectroscopy The process of identifying materials by the way they absorb or emit particular frequencies of electromagnetic radiation.

Steel An alloy of iron and carbon. (Usually containing up to about 1.5 to 2% carbon.) Specialist steels may contain other alloying elements like chromium or tungsten to impart specific properties.

Steroid A group of complex alcohols that include the sex hormone testosterone and the substance cholesterol.

Straight chain The arrangement of carbon atoms in organic molecules in which all the carbon atoms are in a straight chain with no branching.

Strong acid An acid which is almost 100% ionised.

Strong base A base which is almost 100% ionised.

Structural formula A way of displaying the formula of a compound so that the bonds and the approximate positions of the atoms are shown. Usually only used for organic compounds.

Temporary hardness Water hardness that can be removed by boiling the water. Usually caused by calcium or magnesium hydrogen carbonate.

Thermal decomposition The breaking down of a compound by the action of heat.

Thermosetting plastics Polymers which have to be heated to make them cure (set).

Thermosoftening plastics Polymers that soften when heated and can be moulded into shape.

Titration A method of determining the concentration of a solution by neutralising it with another solution of known concentration.

Transition elements The name given to the elements in the Periodic Table between Groups 2 and 3.

Transition metal See transition elements.

Unsaturated hydrocarbons Hydrocarbons in which some of the carbon atoms are linked together with C = C double bonds.

Water cycle The process by which water on the Earth circulates. Water in the sea evaporates into the air. It cools and falls back as precipitation (e.g. rain).

Water of crystallisation The water contained within the crystals of some substances.

Weak acid An acid which is almost totally unionised.

Weak base A base which is almost totally unionised.

Wrought iron Almost pure iron.

Yeast A naturally-occurring microorganism that produces enzymes that cause fermentation.

Index

Note: Glossary entries are in bold.

Photo acknowledgements

The publishers would like to thank the following individuals, institutions and companies for permission to reproduce photographs in this book. Every effort has been made to trace ownership of copyright. The publishers would be happy to make arrangements with any copyright holder whom it has not been possible to contact:

Andrew Lambert (2, 6 bottom, 25 bottom, 47 bottom, 54, 55, 56, 67 all, 68 all, 69); GSF Picture Library (53 bottom left & right); Hodder and Stoughton (29 top left); Library and Reference Centre, Royal Society of Chemistry (48 left); Life File (6 top, 17, 30 all, 32, 37, 41 all, 42 top left & right); Martin Sookias Photography (26 all, 47 top left & right, 70 top); Poeton (Gloucester) Ltd (27); RD Battersby (13, 25 top, 42 bottom); The Royal Library, Copenhagen (48 right); Ruth Nossek (1); Science Photo Library (24, 28 top right & bottom, 29, 31, 36, 38, 39 all, 45, 52 bottom, 70 bottom left & right, 72); Stuart Wilson (51 all, 52 top, 53 top).

Orders: please contact Bookpoint Ltd, 130 Milton Park, Abingdon, Oxon OX14 4SB.
Telephone: (44) 01235 827720, Fax: (44) 01235 400454. Lines are open from 9.00–6.00, Monday to Saturday, with a 24 hour message answering service. Email address: orders@bookpoint.co.uk

British Library Cataloguing in Publication Data
A catalogue record for this title is available from The British Library

ISBN 0 340 84782 4

First published 2002
Impression number   10 9 8 7 6 5 4 3 2 1
Year   2008 2007 2006 2005 2004 2003 2002

Copyright © 2002 Terry Mansfield

Cover illustration by Sarah Jones, Debut Art
Typeset by J&L Composition Ltd, Filey, North Yorkshire.
Printed in Italy for Hodder & Stoughton Educational, a division of Hodder Headline Plc, 338 Euston Road, London NW1 3BH.